Favorite Paintings from the

CINCINNATI ART MUSEUM

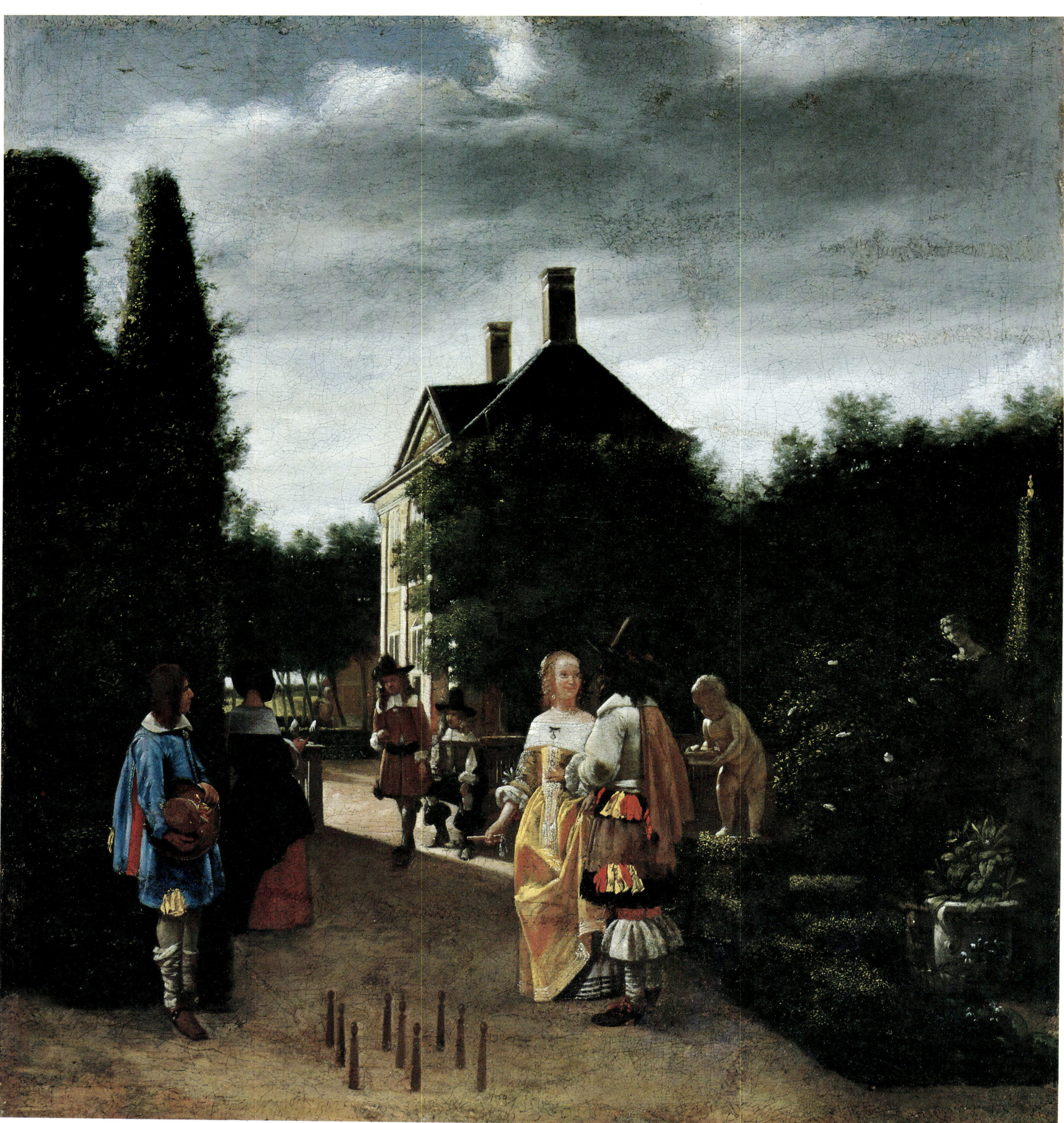

Favorite Paintings from the
CINCINNATI ART MUSEUM

By Millard F. Rogers, Jr.
Director, Cincinnati Art Museum

ABBEVILLE PRESS • PUBLISHERS • NEW YORK

ON THE FRONT COVER:
The Rumanian Blouse by Henri Matisse

FACING THE TITLE PAGE:
The Game of Skittles by Pieter de Hooch

ON THE BACK COVER:
Italian Girl with Fan by John Singer Sargent

ACKNOWLEDGMENTS

The talent and expertise of several staff members of the Cincinnati Art Museum contributed to the preparation of this book. The assistance of the following individuals is gratefully acknowledged by the author: (editing) Betty L. Zimmerman; (typing and editorial assistance) Carol M. Schoellkopf; (photography coordination) Beth DeWall; (photography) Ron Forth; (gallery assistance) Edward Farrell; (conservation) Elisabeth Batchelor, Lance Mayer, Gay Myers.

MILLARD F. ROGERS, JR.

Library of Congress Cataloging in Publication Data

Cincinnati. Art Museum.
Fifty favorite paintings in the Cincinnati Art Museum.

1. Painting—Ohio—Cincinnati. 2. Cincinnati. Art Museum. I. Rogers, Millard F. II. Title.
N550.A58 750'.74'017178 80-17245
ISBN 0-89659-159-X

CONTENTS

INTRODUCTION

By Millard F. Rogers, Jr.

Director, Cincinnati Art Museum

IN THE EARLY NINETEENTH CENTURY, Cincinnati became a surging center for manufacturing, commerce, and transportation, and by 1850 it was the largest city west of the Alleghenies. Wealth and arts patronage go hand-in-hand, and Cincinnati had both. Many artists were attracted to this "Queen City," as Longfellow called it, by the art schools that offered instruction, by the growing number of galleries and exhibition possibilities, and by the patrons and collectors. Dr. Daniel Drake's Western Museum of natural history and art, founded in 1818, was typical for its times in its blend of curiosities, art objects, and specimens. The exotic presentations by its curator, Joseph Dorfeuille, who concocted dioramas and mechanically activated displays, and Mrs. Frances Trollope's bazaar ("Trollope's Folly") of 1829-1830 may have contributed somewhat to the pretensions to a cultural climate in Cincinnati. A short-lived "Academy of Fine Arts" was formed by Frederick Eckstein, the sculptor, in 1826, and Letton's Museum operated between 1818 and 1836, exhibiting fifty painted portraits of local citizens.(In 1828, Frederick Franks opened a "gallery of fine arts," and he was the operator who continued the Western Museum and its "infernal regions" (the displays made by Dorfeuille and Hiram Powers) until 1853. But none of these were art museums, and their influence on painters and painting was hardly significant.

As early as 1838 the Cincinnati Academy of Fine Arts, with a membership composed of professional artists and amateurs, was organized to provide lessons, collections, and exhibitions. The Western Art Union followed in 1847, devoting itself to the purchase of American art to be sold by lottery. The Ladies' Academy of Fine Arts, formed under the leadership of the remarkable Mrs. Sarah Worthington King Peter in 1854, attempted the "improvement of the public taste, and the encouragement of art." Works of art collected by this association included copies of old master paintings, and these formed the city's earliest intact group of pictures that could be called a public collection.

Among the earliest painters in the Queen City were James H. Beard, T. Worthington Whittredge, the brothers John and Godfrey Frankenstein, Miner K. Kellogg, William Sonntag, Thomas Buchanan Read, and Joseph Oriel Eaton. Cincinnati's most famous sculptor, Hiram Powers, preceded these artists early in the nineteenth century and received much-needed support from Nicholas Longworth (1782-1863), a patron who helped many, including Robert Duncanson, America's foremost black artist. Certainly Longworth, who amassed his wealth in real estate, was the outstanding patron and collector in the first half of the nineteenth century. He owned a canvas by Benjamin West, *Ophelia and Laertes*, painted about 1792, that may well be the first important oil painting to have moved beyond the eastern seaboard in the western expansion. It is now in the Cincinnati Art Museum's collection and was one of its first painting acquisitions (1882). Other early collectors and patrons of significance were Reuben R. Springer and Charles Stetson, the latter an organizer of the Western Art Union. The Museum's painting collection is rich in works by Cincinnati artists supported by these and other collectors. As a corporation and building, the Museum is indebted to their generosity and interest.

In 1877, fresh from their successful exhibition at the Centennial Exposition in Philadelphia, a group organized around Cincinnati's women art potters formed the Women's Art Museum Association. A fund was started in 1878 to establish a museum, and temporary exhibition quarters were put to frequent use. In 1880, Charles West offered $150,000 to found a museum if matching funds could be raised. This was done in a month's time. The Cincinnati Art Museum was incorporated on February 15, 1881, and one year later the City of Cincinnati deeded nineteen acres in Eden Park as a museum site, where a Romanesque Revival-style edifice opened to the public in May, 1886, the "Art Palace of the West," as one reviewer called it. Over the years, several wings have been added to enlarge the Museum, providing extensive exhibition space for the permanent collection and temporary shows.

Although the avowed purpose of the Women's Art Museum Association was to fund a museum that would "encourage the application of the principles of art and science to manufacturing and practical life," this concept never restricted the Cincinnati Art Museum in fashioning itself after the leading model for decorative and applied art museums, the Victoria & Albert Museum in London. Paintings and a variety of art objects were collected even before the Museum opened in 1886, casting the mold for its becoming a general art museum that would span ancient to modern times in its collection.

Even before the Cincinnati Art Museum was incorporated, paintings had been collected specifically for it, although none of these works would be considered worthy of a major museum and they are not now exhibited. The first painting to be accessioned in the Museum's collection was a copy of Raphael's *School of Athens* (1881). Paintings by Carl F. Lessing, Emanuel Leutze, Eastman Johnson, and Andreas Achenbach followed in 1882. Since then, the collection of paintings has grown by gift, bequest, and purchase. The character of the collection was not designed, but the generosity of donors and well-reasoned purchases have combined over many decades to form a balanced collection that represents medieval to modern painting capped by world-renowned masterpieces. Today the Museum's painting collection represents a significant portion of its holdings and exhibited objects, with a range of medieval to contemporary works.

The earliest major bequest of paintings brought with it an endowment for additional acquisitions when John J. Emery, Sr., died in 1910. His bequest stipulated that ". . . as Art has no nationality, the products of the artists of any country shall not have a preference." Since 1910, the Emery endowment has acquired works by El Greco, Tiepolo, Trumbull, and Cassatt, among others. In 1924 and 1978 the bequest of Mr. and Mrs. Walter J. Wichgar transferred many American paintings to the Museum to enlarge the extensive holdings given in 1915 and earlier by Frank Duveneck, Cincinnati's distinguished artist and teacher.

The magnificent bequest of paintings by Mary M. Emery in 1927 concluded a lifetime of patronage and support for the Cincinnati Art Museum and represents only a small part of this remarkable lady's generosity and concern for a wide range of charitable and civic causes. Mrs. Emery's collection of paintings remains today the important nucleus of the Museum's old masters.

Several benefactors bequeathed acquisition funds for paintings although they themselves were not collectors. Fanny Bryce Lehmer was one of these, and since her death in 1936 her endowment has become one of the major funds for enrichment of the painting collection. In 1940, the Museum was given an outstanding group of paintings by Emilie L. Heine, with the donor retaining life interest until her death in 1949. There were nearly fifty paintings in this prestigious group of French, Dutch, and English works, led by an impressive representation of the Barbizon School, including twelve works by Corot and examples by Millet, Rousseau, and Daubigny. In 1943, the Museum received the Harry S. and Eva Belle Leyman collection, with the famous Benson Madonna by Botticini included in this gift. Miss Mary Hanna was a faithful, generous patron of the Museum for many decades, beginning with her gift of a Sorolla painting in 1910. While most of her collection of over thirty oil paintings was presented in 1946, with superb examples by Claude, Constable, Ruisdael, and De Hooch, she bequeathed an equally superb group of watercolors and pastels at her death in 1956, plus the largest financial bequest ever received.

Another major financial bequest was received from Mrs. Edwin U. Irwin in 1952, establishing the Edwin and Virginia Irwin Memorial for the purchase of paintings. Among notable acquisitions from this fund since 1957 are works by Grant Wood, Honoré Daumier, Guercino, and Hans Hofmann. Joining the other distinguished benefactors who were named "Mary" (Mary M. Emery and Mary Hanna) was a third lady, Mary E. Johnston, who was encouraged in her art interests by her uncle, Colonel William Cooper Procter. Miss Johnston's bequest in 1967 enriched the Museum's holdings of late nineteenth and twentieth-century paintings, contributing works by artists that were not represented before, such as Gris, Chagall, and Arp, and it added major examples by Picasso, Matisse, and other School of Paris masters.

With the publication of this book of fifty selections, the Cincinnati Art Museum marks its Centennial and pays tribute to one hundred years of collecting, exhibiting, preserving, and interpreting paintings in its galleries. The choices were difficult ones, and undoubtedly there are favorites that would have been chosen by others. I have tried to select not only my personal favorites, but also a group of fifty that illustrates recognized masterpieces and reviews the wide range of the painting collection.

ON THE FRONT COVER

Henri Matisse

1869-1954 • FRENCH

The Rumanian Blouse

1937

MATISSE'S LIFE spanned the birth of Impressionism to the onset of Pop Art, from his beginnings as a student of a prominent academician to decorating a chapel at Vence, France, with its startling explosions of color in glass, paint, and textiles. Matisse absorbed the art of the past, and struggled as a young artist, joining a group called the *Fauves* that included Signac, Vlaminck, and Derain. He was encouraged by the writer and collector, Gertrude Stein, who introduced him to other patrons, and by 1910 (just as Cubism and Picasso surged to the front of modern art) he was recognized as a leader of contemporary painting. His influences came from exotic sources, such as North Africa, giving him a never-flagging concern for flat, two-dimensional shapes, color, and fluid line.

Costumes fascinated Matisse. His models frequently were posed in elaborate fabrics and placed against backgrounds of tropical foliage. By at least 1935, Matisse began a series of drawings of a model wearing a richly embroidered Rumanian blouse, a theme that obsessed him until 1940 and later. In the Cincinnati painting the artist blended bright color, sensitive line, and a perception for abstraction that fused all elements into one glorious design. The resulting pattern that Matisse created, no matter how accidental or casual some elements may appear, carefully stated his vision of what painting should be.

Oil on canvas, 28¾ x 23⅝"
Bequest of Mary E. Johnston, 1967

Master of San Baudelio

ACTIVE MID-12TH CENTURY • SPANISH

The Falconer

c. 1125-1150

FAR OUT IN THE BROWN, barren, and gently rolling hills of Soria province in Spain, a small stone church was built in the eleventh century to commemorate a site associated with San Baudelio, a fourth-century martyr. Its walls and ceiling were decorated lavishly with frescoes (paintings executed with wet pigments on plaster) a century later, to depict incidents from the life of the Virgin and Christ along with scenes from events pertaining to Saints Baudelio and Nicholas. The artist is unknown, which is typical of the anonymity of craftsmen in the Romanesque period.

The Falconer is conceived in a flat design, in stark color and bold shapes, and portrayed as an armed knight on horseback. He pursues the medieval pastime of falconry that was an essential part of the hunt. This section was once part of a lower frieze of hunting scenes, an attractive group of secular, chivalrous activities that related the contemporary twelfth-century worshiper to the Christian themes painted higher up on vaulted ceiling and walls.

Paintings of the twelfth century are rare and seldom seen outside their originally intended locations in churches and secular buildings. The Cincinnati fresco, along with most of the painted decoration, was removed from the Ermita de San Baudelio and sold by the villager-owners decades ago. The series is the finest example of Spanish Romanesque fresco painting in America. At the Cincinnati Art Museum, this painting and seven others from the same fresco cycle may be seen in a reconstruction of the tiny church and its apse that once was decorated with these handsome works.

Fresco transferred to canvas, 86⅝ x 78⅞"
Gift of Elijah B. Martindale and Edwin and Virginia Irwin Memorial, 1962-1964

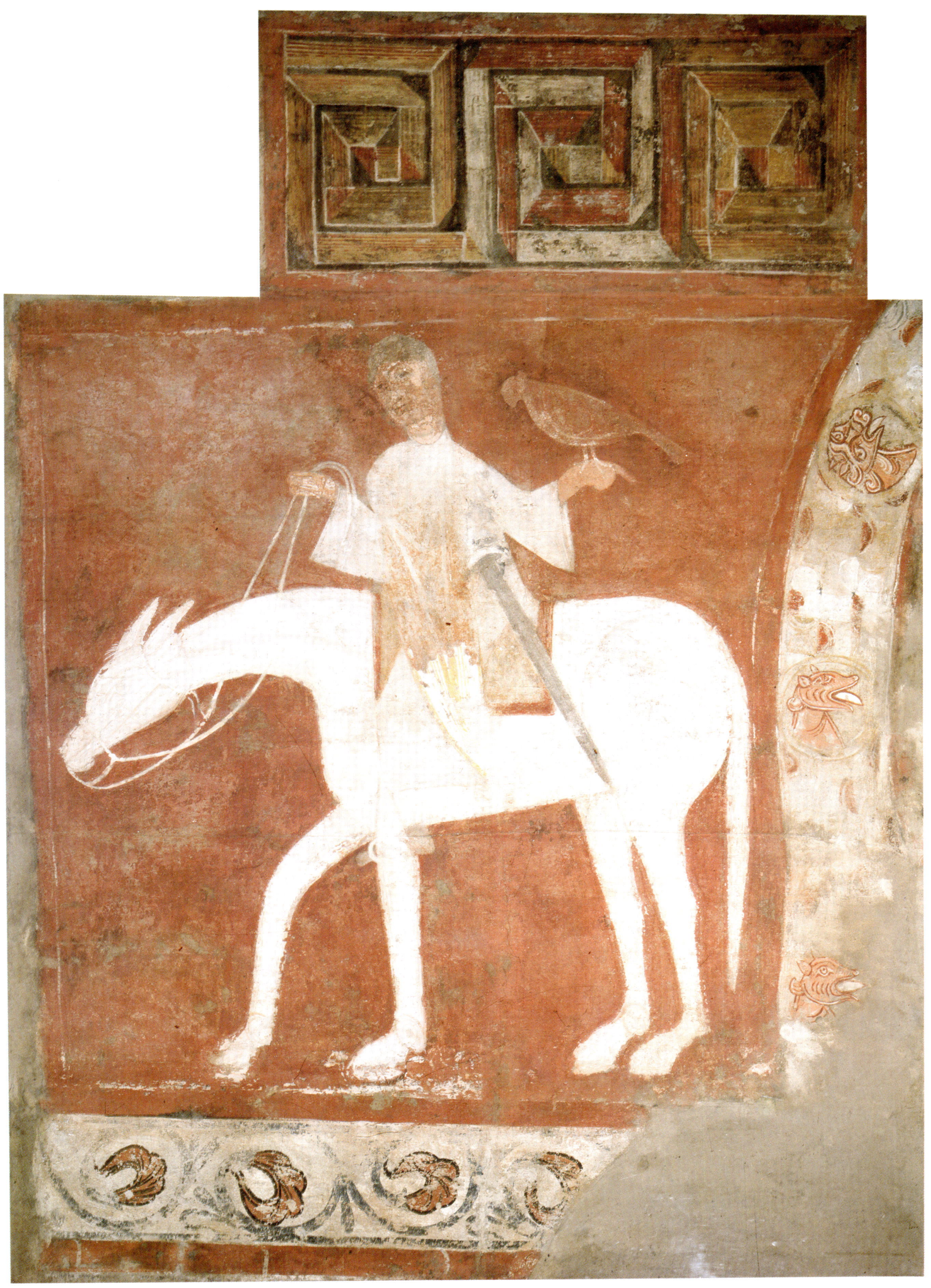

Andrea Mantegna

1431-1506 • ITALIAN

Esther and Mordecai

c. 1500-1505

VICENZA WAS THE CITY OF MANTEGNA'S BIRTH, not far from Padua and Venice. His early training was with Squarcione. The artistic giants of the fifteenth century whom Mantegna must have known included Donatello and the Bellini family of Venice. During his training in Padua, Mantegna's fascination with antique Roman art was formed, a devotion he never lost. He utilized antique elements frequently in his paintings, such as the classical relief carving depicted at right behind Mordecai. In 1459, Mantegna moved with his family to the Gonzaga court at Mantua, where he remained for the rest of his life except for journeys he made to Rome and Florence.

In the *Book of Esther* is the story of the beautiful Israelite winning the favor of the Persian king Ahasuerus and ultimately saving her people with the help of her cousin Mordecai, who is shown here discussing the decree that ordered the death of the Jews. Mordecai is shown in sackcloth and with an unkempt beard, standing before the palace portal and the queen. The scene is painted *en grisaille*, a palette limited to earth colors touched with gold to delineate the two figures as if they were sculptured from crisp metal.

The collection of Museum benefactor Mary Muhlenberg Emery included no greater masterpiece than this priceless work from the Renaissance. America's greatest period of art collecting occurred in the decade just before and after World War I. Europe's country houses and noble collections relinquished many treasures to aggressive dealers like Duveen who acquired Cincinnati's Mantegna from the Duke of Buccleuch and then sold it to Mrs. Emery.

Oil on canvas, 22⅛ x 19⅛"
Bequest of Mary M. Emery, 1927

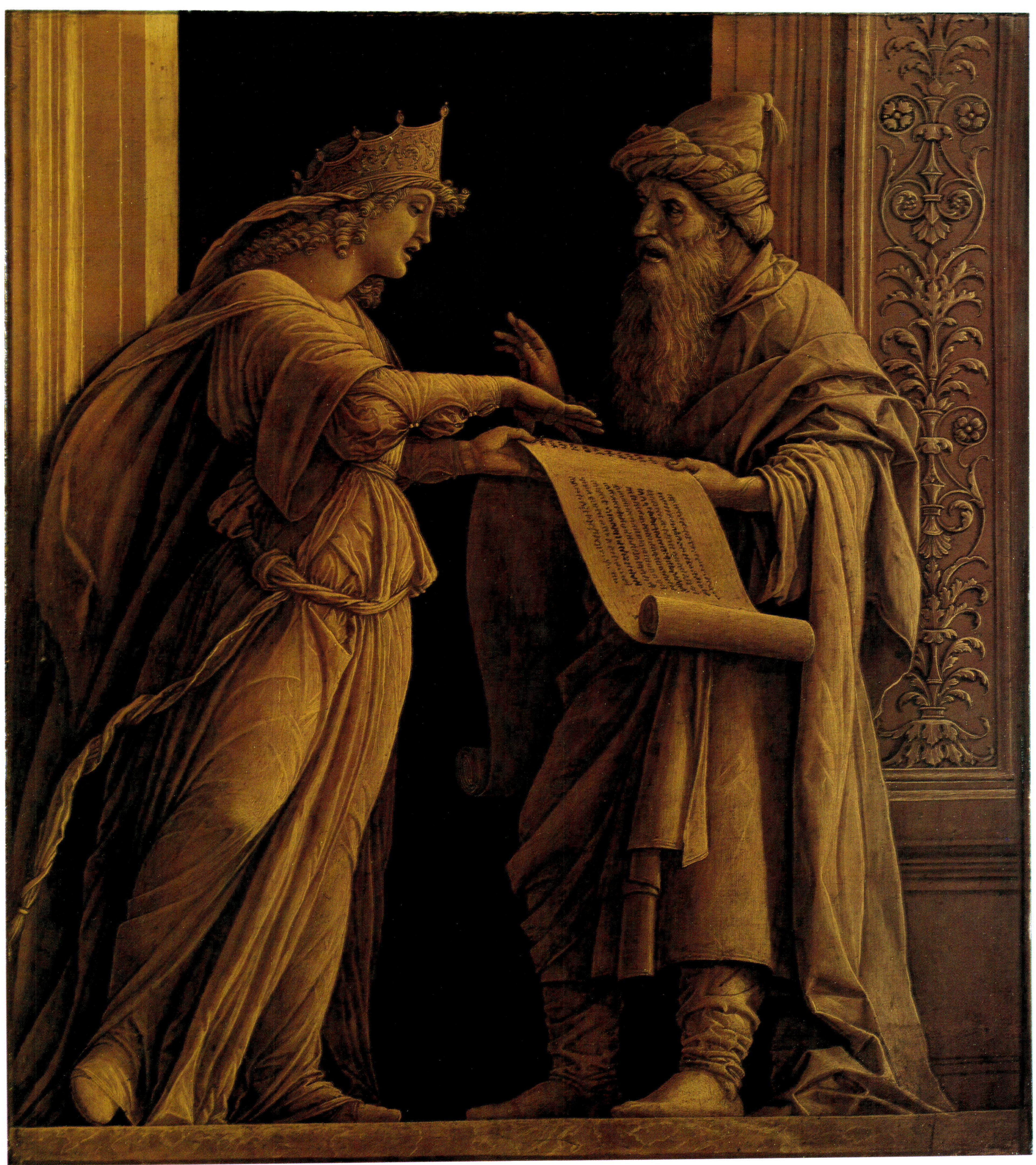

Hans Memling

c. 1433-1494 • FLEMISH

St. Stephen and *St. Christopher*

c. 1480

IN THE FIFTEENTH CENTURY, Flanders was a cultural and political complex that included most of present-day Holland, Belgium, Luxembourg, and considerable land in the Burgundy and Lorraine regions of France. Its principal cities—Antwerp, Brussels, Bruges, Ghent, and Dijon—were wealthy commercial centers. The dukes of Burgundy ruled Flanders and established order and security in the provinces they drew together; by the fifteenth century a prosperous, enlightened national entity was forged. Patronage of the arts flourished.

Hans Memling is but one of several exceptionally gifted painters of the Flemish Renaissance that included Jan van Eyck, Hugo van der Goes, Hieronymus Bosch, Gerard David, and Rogier van der Weyden. Memling was active in Bruges, one of Europe's most civilized cities and a banking center of highest rank. He joined the Painter's Guild, a union of professional artists, by 1468. His principal patrons were the bourgeois of Bruges and its colony of foreign businessmen, mostly Italians.

These two paintings once were part of an altarpiece now dismembered (two panels from the same polyptych are in the Louvre), and they have a history of noble ownership that included Napoleon Bonaparte and his brother, Lucien; King William II of Holland; and the grand dukes of Saxe-Weimar. In these delicately painted panels, episodes shown in the landscape backgrounds illustrate the martyrdoms of the two saints. Memling's precise technique owed much of its jewel-like colors and attention to detail to influences from illuminated manuscripts of the same century and earlier.

Oil and tempera on oak panels, (St. Stephen) 18 23/32 x 6 3/16", (St. Christopher) 18 13/16 x 6 5/32"
Gift of Mrs. E. W. Edwards, 1955, 1956

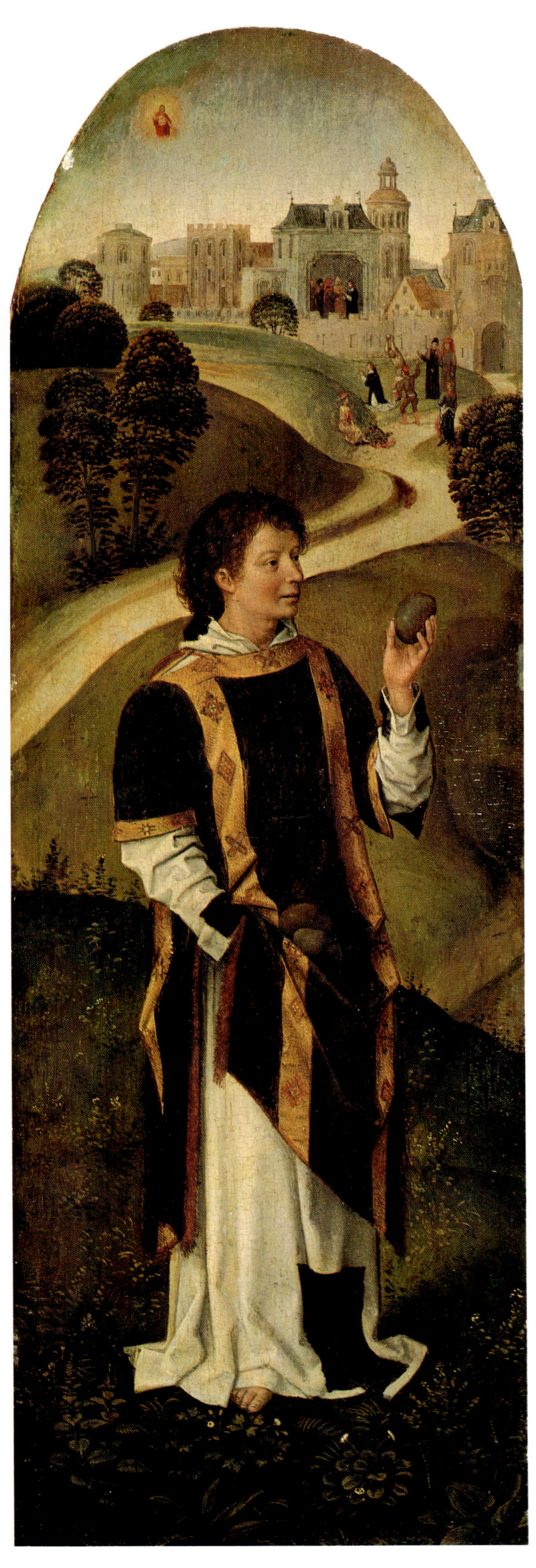

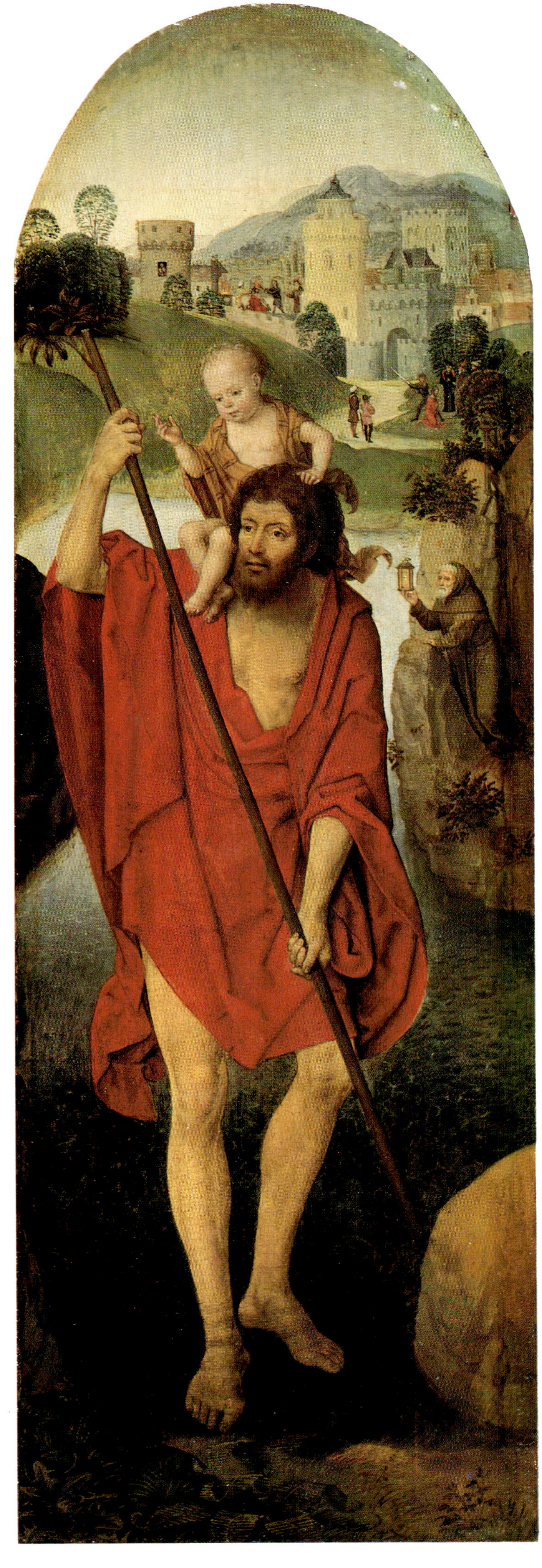

Sandro Botticelli

(ALESSANDRO DI MARIANO DEI FILIPEPI) c. 1445-1510 • ITALIAN

Judith with the Head of Holofernes

c. 1468-1469

STRIDING RESOLUTELY FORWARD with only a slight backward glance at her maid, a woman with sword in one hand and a wispy olive branch in the other has completed her grisly mission. In the Apocrypha's *Book of Judith*, the legend is told of the Assyrians' siege of Bethulia and the visits to their camp by a young Jewish woman, Judith, and her maid who carried a basket of food with her each day. Gaining the confidence of Holofernes, the Assyrian general, on the fourth visit Judith beheaded Holofernes and departed from the enemy camp with her servant carrying the trophy of the daring act. The scene was popular in the fifteenth century as an example of feminine virtue and the accomplishment of a righteous cause.

Painted in the most delicate tones and with the expressive angularity that makes Botticelli's figures appear sculptured from metal, this panel is like a miniature in its sensitive design and finish, obviously meant for contemplation and private enjoyment. It has the same delicacy and subtle coloring of the other, well-known (but slightly later) version of this subject in the Uffizi, Florence. The Cincinnati painting probably preceded the Uffizi version by a year or two and is more correctly titled *The Return of Judith to Bethulia*. A remarkable composition on the panel's reverse side showing two deer and two monkeys is the only known painting by Botticelli without human figures.

Botticelli (known by a nickname meaning "little barrel") was apprenticed to Fra Lippo Lippi in 1459-1467 and may have worked with Verrocchio who also was the teacher of Leonardo da Vinci. Botticelli's home was Florence, a cultural center in the fifteenth century unlike any the world has ever seen, and there he painted until sometime about 1500 when he was swayed by the reforms of Savonarola and probably curtailed his output considerably, if he did not cease to paint altogether.

Oil and tempera on panel, 11 5/16 x 8 1/4"
J. J. Emery Endowment, 1954

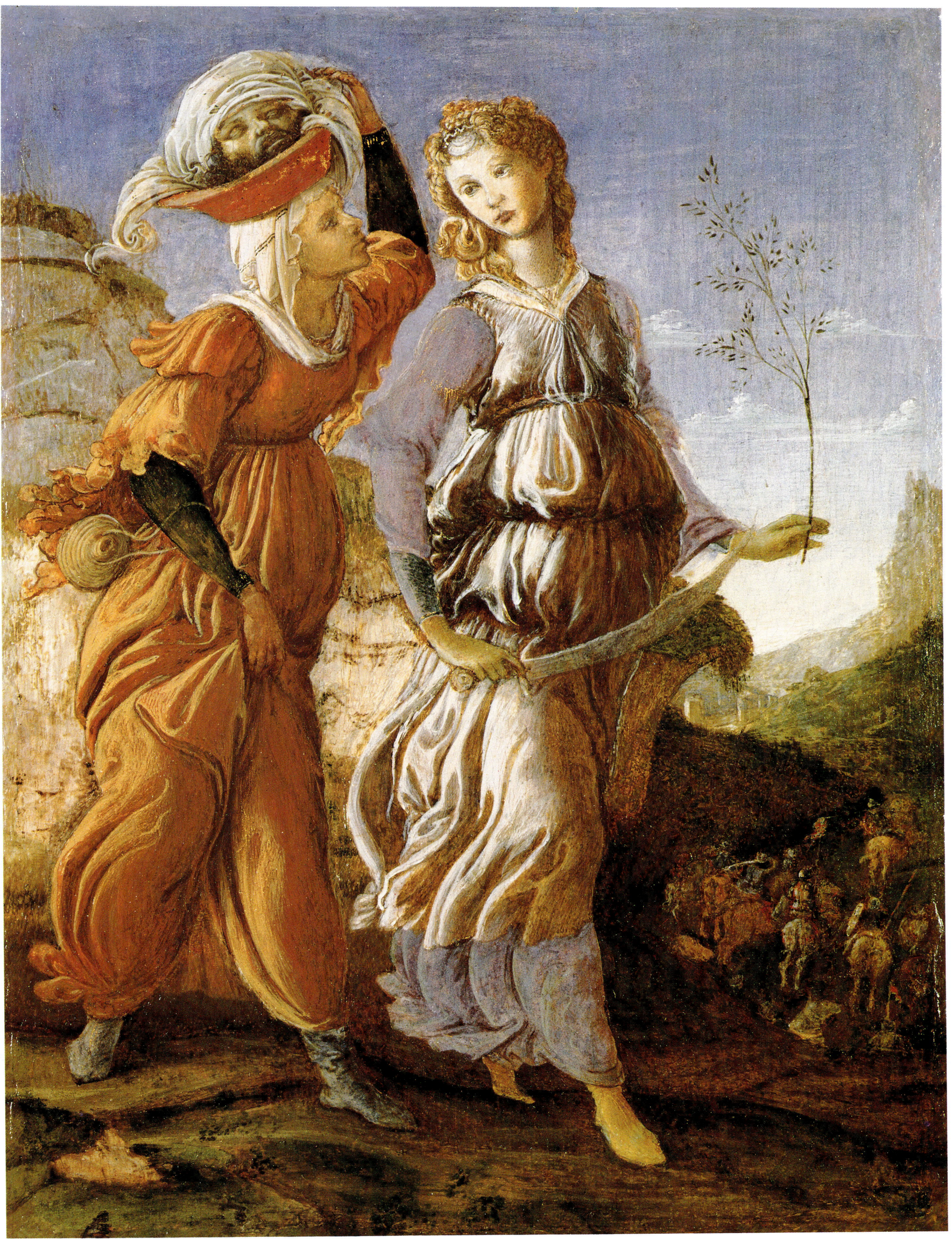

Titian

(TIZIANO VECELLI) c. 1488-1576 • ITALIAN

Philip II

c. 1549-1551

TITIAN WAS A STUDENT with Gentile Bellini but was influenced largely in his youth by Giorgione, also Venetian. By 1512, Titian was established as the leading painter in Venice. His very personal style was considered "modern" when compared with the reserved Renaissance works of the fifteenth century, and this endeared him to his Venetian patrons. The emperor Charles V called him to Bologna in 1532, and following this meeting with the most powerful monarch in the world, Titian became the emperor's court painter. His career was long, his production prolific, and Titian's paintings represent the richness and importance of the Venetian School better than any other artist's. In the entire history of painting, Titian is ranked among the greatest masters.

Titian was summoned to Augsburg in 1548-1549 and again in 1550-1551 to paint the portrait of the heir to the Holy Roman emperor Charles V. The sitter was Philip II, then in his early twenties, and Titian painted this full-scale sketch, called a *modello,* from which other official portraits were to be made. The Hapsburg face and a few other parts of the composition are finished, while the hands, the staff held in Philip's right hand, and details of the costume are blocked in to suggest the pose and its structure. So dependent was Titian on the painting taken from life that he kept it in his studio until his death, using it as the model for all his later court portraits of Philip II. Titian's portraits of these years established the type of official representation that was emulated later by Rubens, Van Dyck, and Velázquez.

Philip (1527-1598) was the son of Charles V and Isabella of Portugal; he was born when Spain was center of the largest empire the world had seen. Throughout Philip's reign, colonization of the New World reached fever pitch; wars with Spain's Protestant enemies (and even against Catholic countries like Italy) were endless. Religious ferment (this was the age of the Reformation) caused major political upheavals everywhere. Perhaps best known for his authorization of the ill-fated Spanish Armada (1588), Philip II was an autocrat with cultural tastes whose patronage of Titian and many other talented artists was generous.

Oil on canvas, 42 3/16 x 36 1/2"
Bequest of Mary M. Emery, 1927

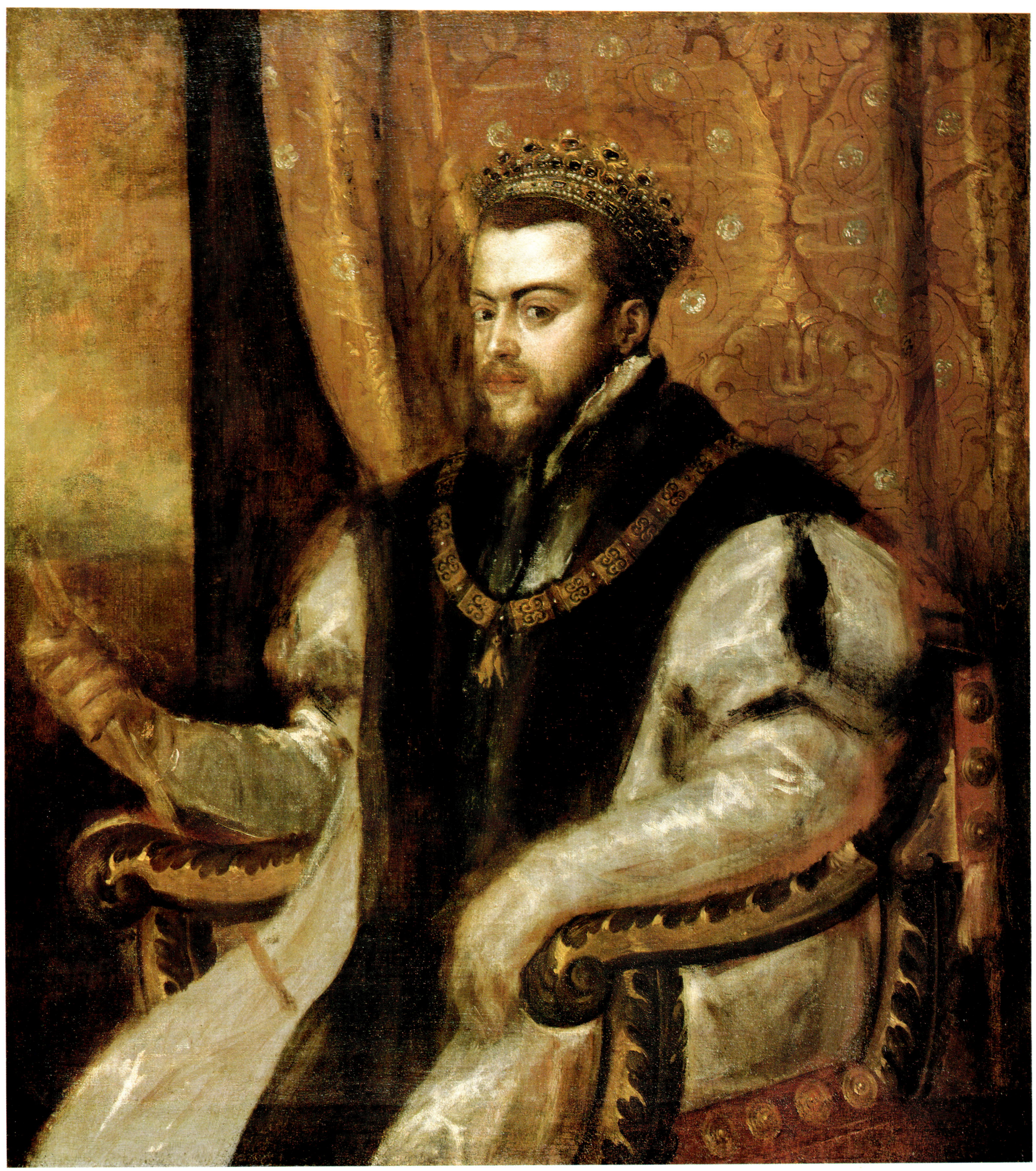

Peter Paul Rubens

1577-1640 • FLEMISH

Samson and Delilah

c. 1609

THE STORY OF SAMSON AND DELILAH from the *Book of Judges* in the Old Testament has been told in verse, music, and art again and again. It is a tale of female allure, seduction, and tragedy. Here Rubens depicts the climactic moment when the superhuman strength of the Bible hero asleep on Delilah's lap was reduced to that of a normal man. As a young Philistine clips the locks that maintained Samson's miraculous strength, soldiers enter at the right to blind the eyes of Samson and shackle him.

This sketch, or *modello,* on wood panel was painted by Rubens as a study for the large, finished version of the same scene that was commissioned in 1609 by the wealthy burgomaster of Antwerp, Nicolaas Rockox, a collector and patron. Preceding the Cincinnati sketch was an ink drawing by Rubens (Van Regteren-Altena Collection, Amsterdam); it and the finished painting (National Gallery, London) exist today as well—a remarkable trio illustrating the artist's development of the theme in three separate stages. The three works are helpful in appreciating the creative process for most artists in the seventeenth century.

Rubens, one of the true masters of painting, was a precocious artist, well trained in Antwerp, well traveled throughout Europe, and equally at ease with paintbrush or diplomatic assignment. Working in Mantua, Rome, London, Antwerp, and elsewhere, Rubens was the major promoter of the Counter-Reformation in painting, the antithesis of Rembrandt and other artists identified with Protestantism. The Baroque period produced many outstanding painters, but none superior to Rubens. His art was passionately theatrical in style and his brushwork identified him as a virtuoso.

Oil on panel, 20½ x 19⅞"
Mr. and Mrs. Harry S. Leyman Endowment, 1972

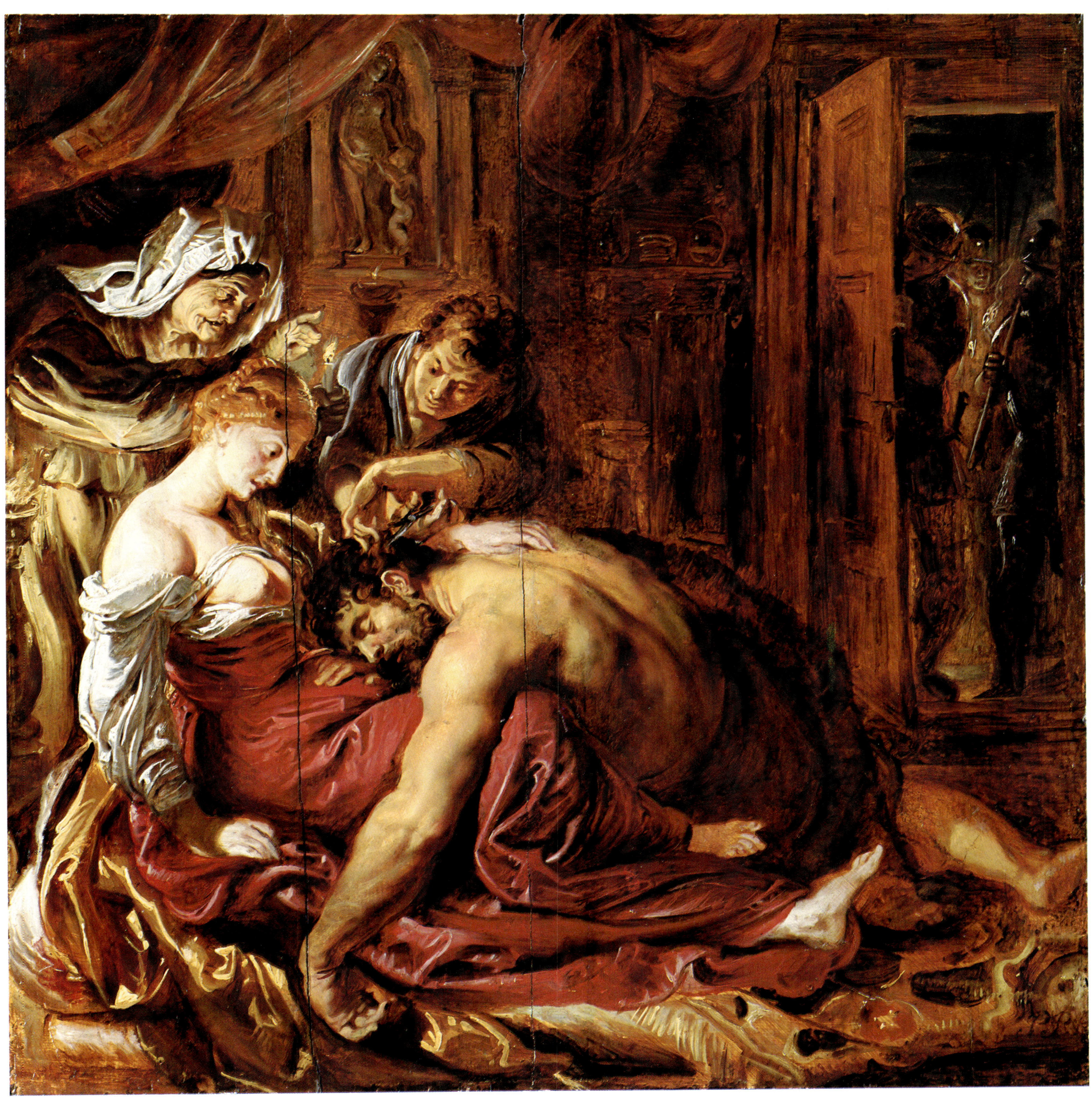

Frans Hals

c. 1580-1666 • DUTCH

A Dutch Family

c. 1635

HALS WAS BORN IN BELGIUM, but he went to Haarlem by 1591 and there he remained for the rest of his life. Like many Dutch artists, Hals was a specialist in one subject, the portrait. And not only did he paint single sitters, but he advanced to perfection the large, life-size civic group portrait depicting guild officers or regents of corporations. These portraits provided the best pay for an artist, and they are a type peculiar to Dutch painting. The Cincinnati group portrait is more intimate in scale and intention, however, than those Hals painted for governors and guilds.

Hals' portraiture, as seen in this vivacious rendering of husband, wife, and two children, always was sympathetic to the models. His sitters seem to exude vitality and joy, and his brushwork was vigorous and sure. He worked directly on canvas with his paints, without preparatory drawings, modeling forms with a virtuosity that has never been surpassed. This unknown and soberly dressed family expresses a joy and self-confidence that Hals readily appreciated, even though his own personal life was anything but happy. Although successful as an artist, Hals was constantly in debt, hounded by creditors, and at the end of his life he was a public charge.

Oil on canvas, 44½ x 36¾″
Bequest of Mary M. Emery, 1927

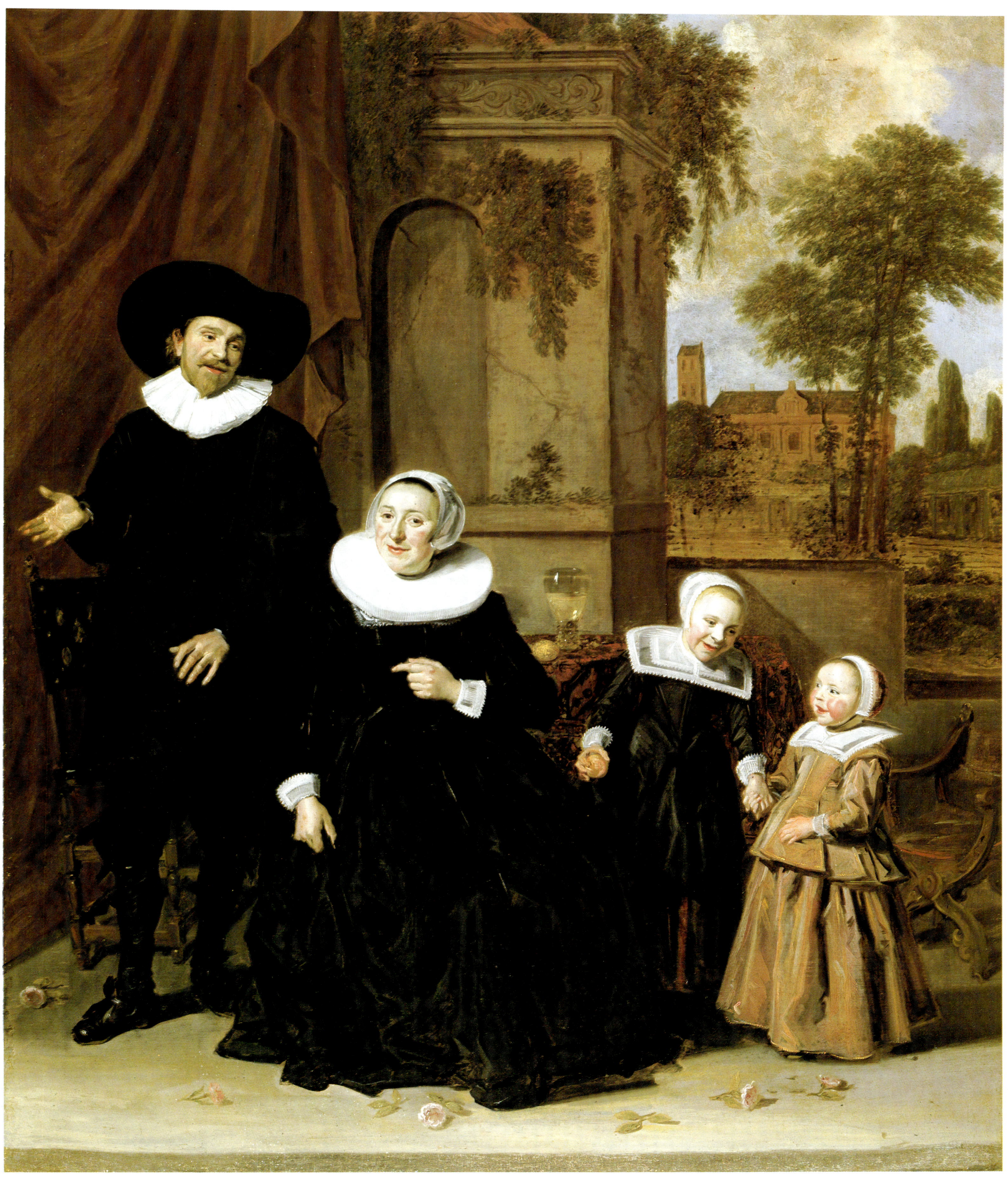

Bernardo Strozzi

1581-1644 • ITALIAN

David with the Head of Goliath

c. 1620-1630

THE ACT IS DONE: David stands grasping his sword and the head of the Philistine Goliath, the Israelite's gaze upturned as if to acknowledge the divine source of his victory against overwhelming odds. The subject was a popular one for Bernardo Strozzi, as several examples in other museums attest; and although the painting is not signed and dated, stylistically it belongs in the early portion of his career.

Strozzi was born in Genoa, the port city, and became a Capuchin friar in 1598. His talents were in engineering as well as painting, for he was port engineer of Genoa for a period before he left for Venice, where he spent the last years of his life from 1631 to 1644. In that Adriatic city he influenced (along with Domenico Fetti and Johann Liss) the painting of Venice's last great painters, Tiepolo and Guardi.

The Baroque movement in the seventeenth century embraced many new attitudes and interests. Strozzi explored, particularly, the realism of Caravaggio and the coloring of Rubens. In this painting's rich colors, its dramatic treatment, in the design of the space with emphatic diagonals (note the beautifully foreshortened arm of David), and in the robust texturing of the paint, this picture is quintessentially Baroque.

Oil on canvas, 60⅜ x 46¼″
J. J. Emery Endowment, 1938

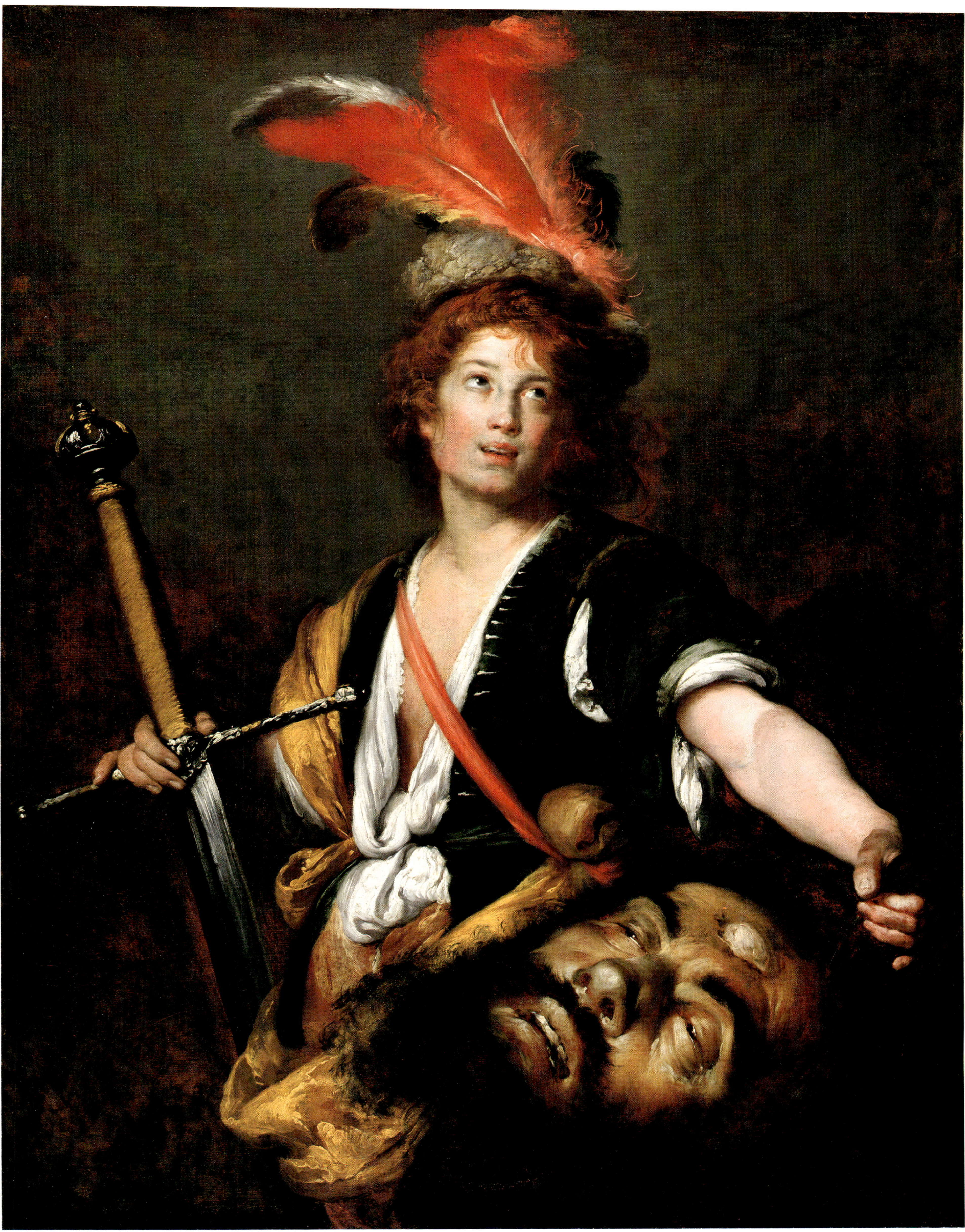

Simon Vouet

1590-1649 • FRENCH

The Toilet of Venus

c. 1628-1639

AT SOME UNKNOWN DATE in this painting's history, probably during the time it hung in one of Cincinnati's distinguished hotels, the nude figure of Venus was overpainted, to drape her body in what someone thought was more demure, more presentable garb. After painstaking cleaning and removing of the overpainting, this splendid rendering of a mythological scene was revealed, showing Venus seated on her marriage couch and gazing into a mirror held by a maid. The scene probably depicts the preparation before Venus' marriage to Vulcan, or it may be a more complicated reference to the death of Vouet's wife in 1638. For whatever purpose, the subject permitted Vouet to organize most dramatically a composition that seems to pulsate with energy (a Baroque characteristic) while expressing a literary subject with decorum, grace, and a talent for depicting life in a superior form.

Simon Vouet's first taste of fame came in Italy where as a young artist he worked in Genoa, Venice, and Rome, even painting a portrait of Pope Urban VIII before being ordered back to France in 1626 as First Painter to the King. In the Louvre of King Louis XIII, which was then a royal palace, several artists worked who subsequently were famous: Charles Lebrun, Eustache Le Sueur, and Pierre Mignard. Vouet introduced the latest Italian fashions in painting, for France was far behind Italy's great Baroque painters with their rich coloring, inventiveness, and idealism. Vouet's primacy with the king was displaced by Poussin by 1642, and in 1649 Vouet died.

Oil on canvas, 72⅜ x 60¼"
Fanny Bryce Lehmer Endowment, 1970

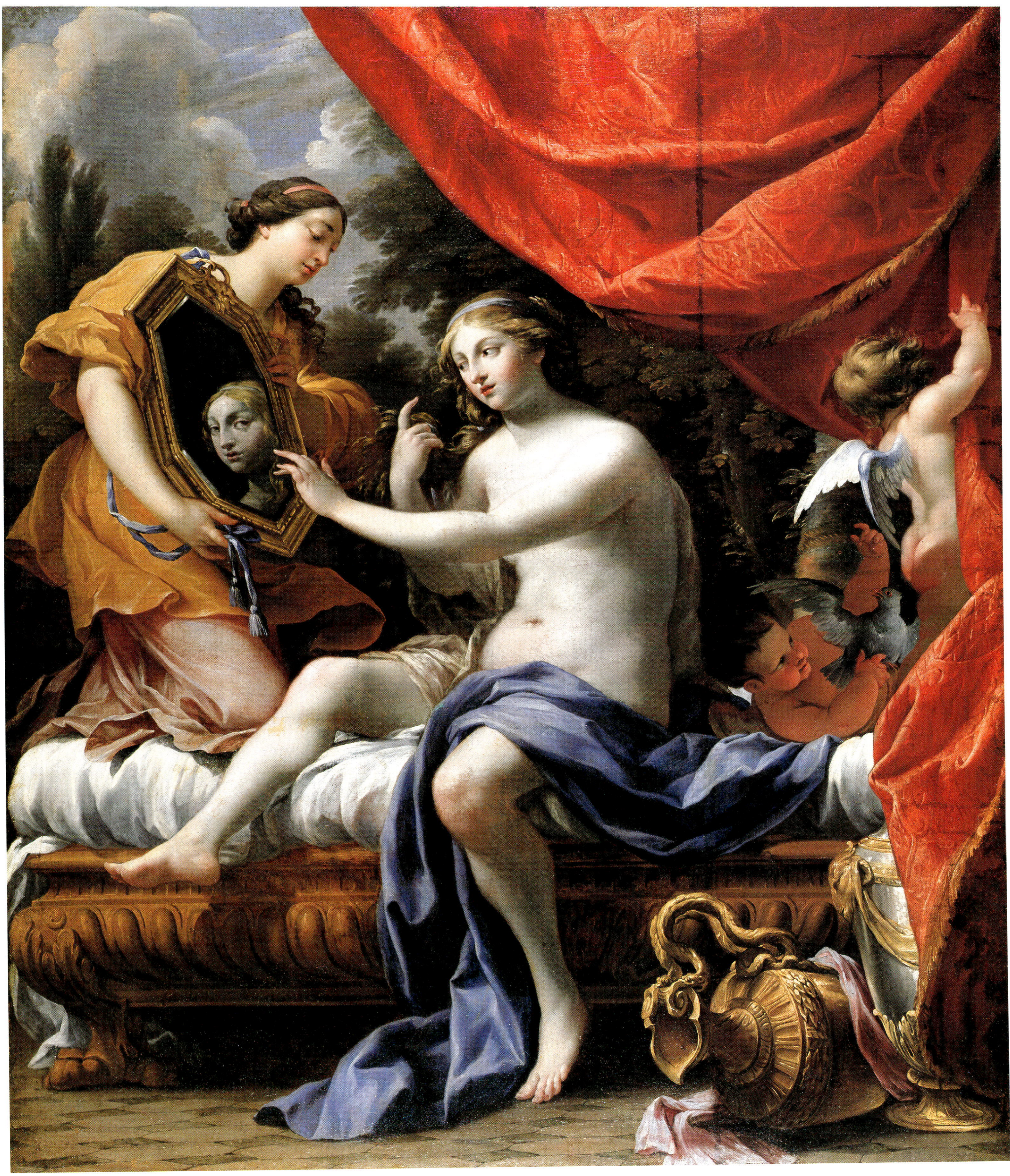

Guercino

(GIOVANNI FRANCESCO BARBIERI) 1591-1666 • ITALIAN

Mars with Cupid

1649

GUERCINO, WHOSE NAME MEANS "SQUINTER," was one of several very talented artists of the Baroque period in seventeenth-century Italy. His career centered largely in Bologna, the north Italian city that fostered such outstanding contemporaries as the Carracci family, Guido Reni, and Domenichino. Not only did Guercino paint easel pictures, but he worked on frescoes, notably the decoration for Pope Gregory XV at the pontiff's Villa Ludovisi in Rome. Guercino enjoyed this patronage until the pope's death in 1623. By 1642, Guercino returned to Bologna. He and Guido Reni had detested each other, and Reni's death allowed Guercino to assume the mantle of the older artist. Back in his home region, Guercino's mature style embraced a dignified monumentality, using concentrated or saturated color to enrich his renderings of mythological and religious objects.

This important painting appears in Guercino's account book, a record of his works kept during his lifetime, listed along with a now-lost pendant depicting Venus, who must have been painted returning the gaze of Mars. The two large-scale paintings were done on commission for an Italian general. The patron's military pursuits are symbolized by Mars, god of war. Mars' love for Venus is suggested by the little cupid holding a heart and arrow.

Oil on canvas, 70 13/16 x 92"
The Edwin and Virginia Irwin Memorial, 1977

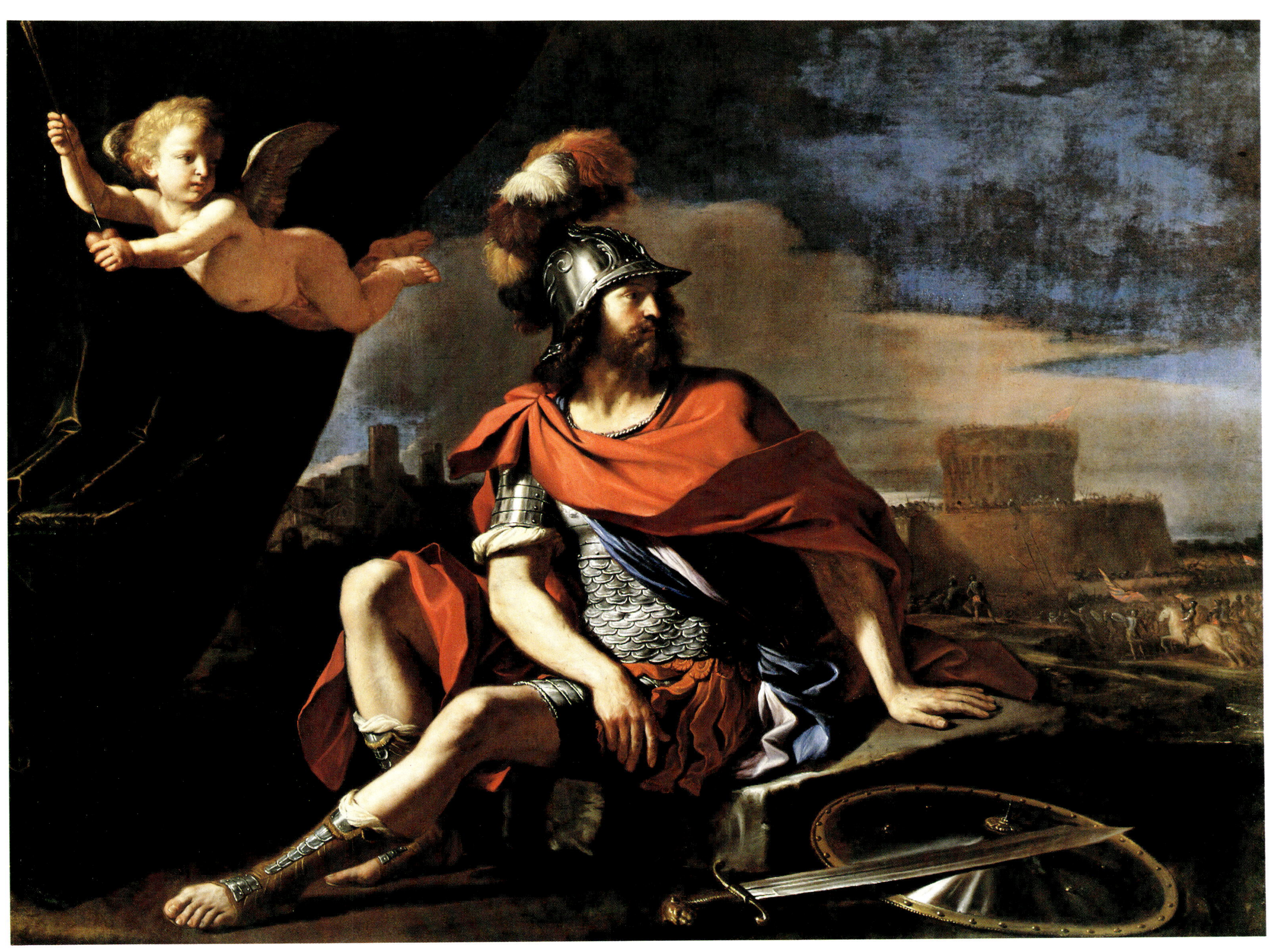

Francisco de Zurbarán

1598-1664 • SPANISH

St. Peter Nolasco Recovering the Image of the Virgin

1630

MORE THAN ANY OTHER SPANISH PAINTER, Zurbarán best expressed the intense faith and religious fervor in Spain in the seventeenth century. He received many commissions for paintings from monasteries and churches. His austere but realistic style appealed particularly to the monastic orders that devoted themselves to prayer, solitude, and the veneration of saints.

In 1628 Zurbarán began to paint a series of twenty-two large canvases dealing with the life of a long-dead saint, Peter Nolasco, for the Convento de la Merced Calzada in Seville. The Cincinnati painting was a part of the series, painted in 1630 as the date on the canvas indicates. It depicts the moment in 1237-1238 when St. Peter Nolasco miraculously directed King James I of Aragón to the location of an image of the Virgin that had been hidden centuries earlier from the invading Moors.

The painting's setting is a shallow space crowded with soldiers, the king, and the saint who clasps his hands in prayer. Looking straight out at the viewer is a boy, thought to be a portrait of the artist's ten-year-old son, Juan, who later became an artist (and is also represented in the Cincinnati Art Museum collection).

There is no proof that Zurbarán ever finished this important series, but at least fifteen of the paintings still existed in the late eighteenth century. The Cincinnati painting, one of about six works remaining today, once belonged to King Louis Philippe of France and was exhibited in his famous gallery of Spanish paintings in the Louvre from 1838 to 1848.

Oil on canvas, 65 1/16 x 82 3/16"
Gift of Miss Mary Hanna, Mr. and Mrs. Charles P. Taft, and Stevenson Scott in Memory of Charles F. Fowles, 1917

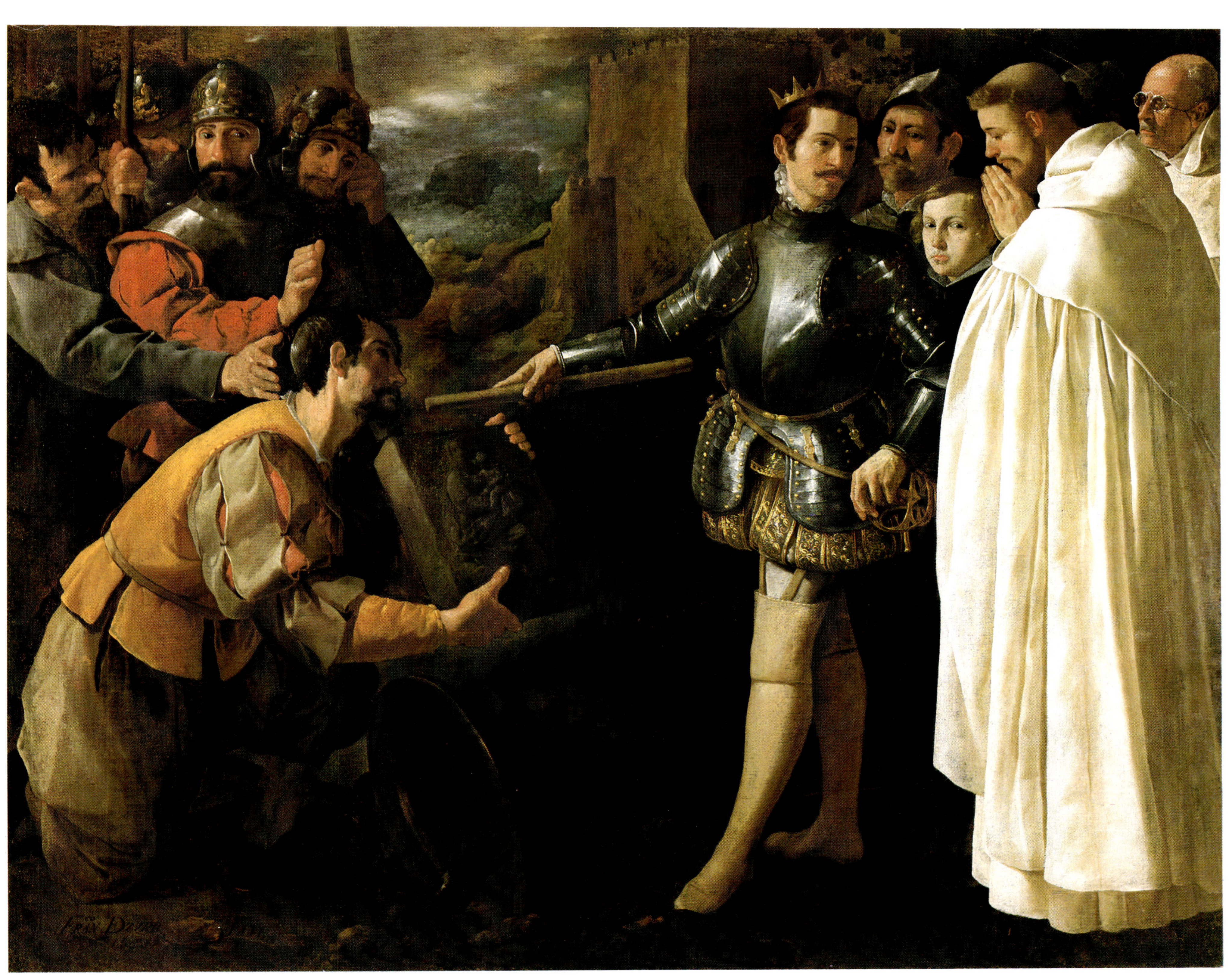

Anthony van Dyck

1599-1641 • FLEMISH

A Member of the Balbi Family

c. 1625

VAN DYCK WAS AS PATRICIAN as his sitters. In his maturity, which he achieved quickly as an artist, he was sought by kings and aristocrats as the greatest portrait painter of his time. No other seventeenth-century artist achieved such fame in a life that spanned only forty-two years, that earned him a knighthood from England's King Charles I and appointment as his court painter, and that saw him travel extensively for commissions in Italy, the Netherlands, and England.

Although Van Dyck was not actually the pupil of Rubens, he became his studio assistant while still a teenager, and in 1618 he became a member of the Antwerp guild of painters. His exceptional facility for capturing a true likeness while investing it with a dramatic, theatrical appearance expresses the essence of the Baroque portrait. From Rubens he learned much about color and brushwork; from Titian, whom he studied in Italy, he absorbed the sense of grandeur that was an element in any portrait he did.

This unknown gentleman in armor grasping the baton that indicates his rank as a general or commander is undoubtedly a member of the Balbi family of Genoa. Van Dyck worked for about five years, 1621-1626, in Italy, confining himself primarily to the coastal city of Genoa where he portrayed the rich and titled Doria, Balbi, and Spinola families. The Cincinnati portrait was seen in the Balbi Palace by one of the seventeenth century's distinguished writers on art, Bellori, and there it remained until it was sold in 1807. Such a portrait usually graced the main salon of a palace, impressing friends and family with the elegance and commanding authority of the sitter, reminding all of the continuity with the past.

Oil on canvas, 52¼ x 47¼"
Bequest of Mary M. Emery, 1927

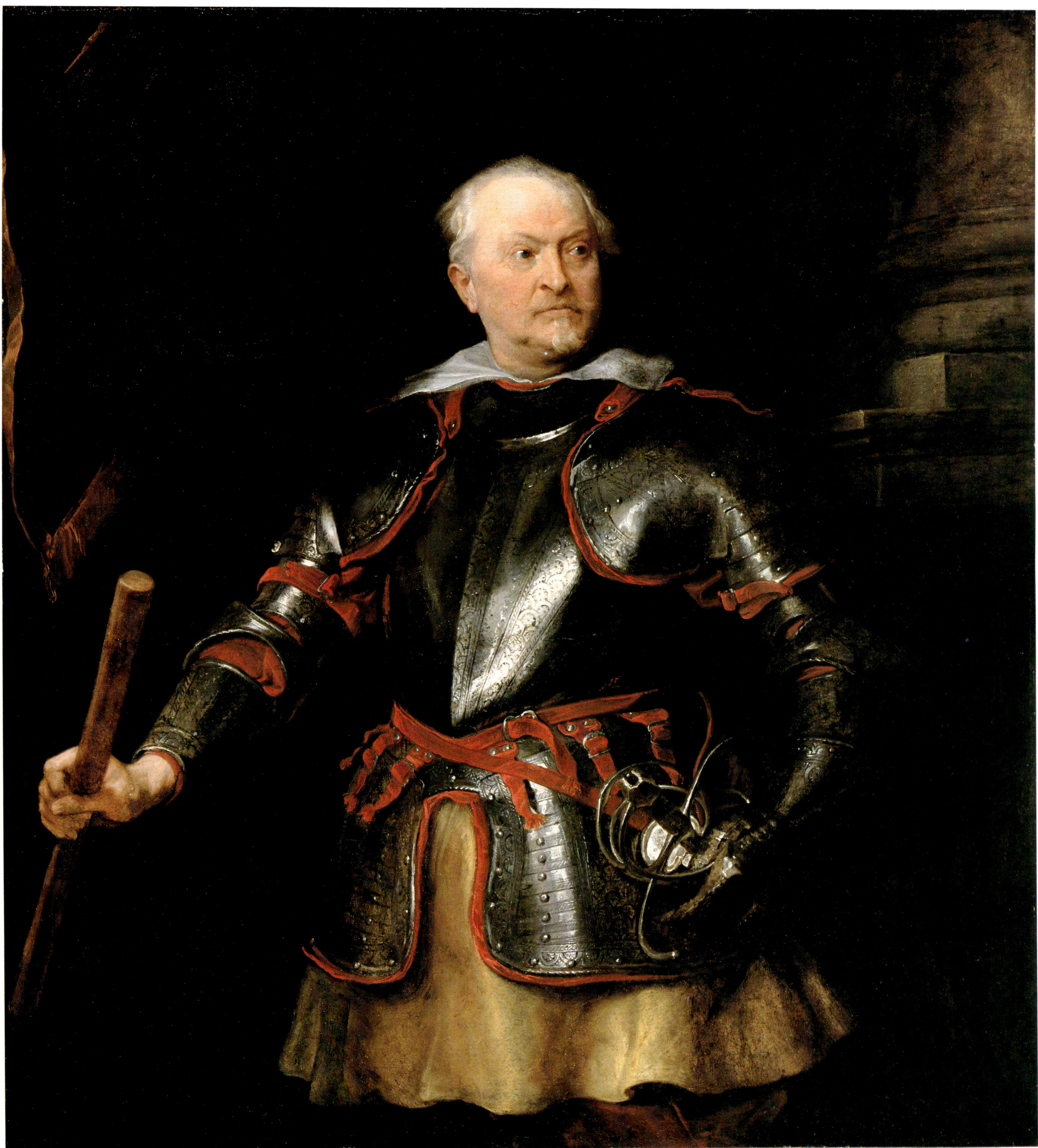

Claude Gellée, called le Lorrain

1600-1682 • FRENCH

Artist Studying from Nature

1639

CLAUDE IS CONSIDERED FRENCH, but he probably spoke the language poorly; he was not well educated, but his paintings seem to derive from the cool, objective mind of an intellectual; and most of his life was spent in Italy as a foreigner. Along with Poussin, he set the style for classicism in French Baroque painting. The paintings of these two masters contrasted sharply with the romantic landscapes of Rembrandt or Jacob van Ruisdael, their contemporary Dutch masters in the seventeenth century.

Rome and its outskirts provided Claude with never-ending subject matter: ancient ruins, peasants tending their flocks, a crystal-clear atmosphere, and sea ports that conjured up the heroic past. Claude developed an especially subtle luminosity that always captured the dawn or the setting sun at the moment when all elements—sketching artist and his friends, boats in harbor, a clump of trees—seem to be blended into a unified whole, a poetically envisioned blend of nature and fantasy.

Claude reproduced two hundred of his paintings as drawings in a collection called *Liber Veritatis*, probably intended to prove his authorship and to serve as a visual catalogue of his works and those who commissioned them. The Cincinnati painting appears in this famous record by Claude as *No. 44, book I*, where it is indicated that it was painted for "M. Perochet," a councilor of Paris and Sêvres.

Oil on canvas, 30¾ x 39¾"
Gift of Mary Hanna, 1946

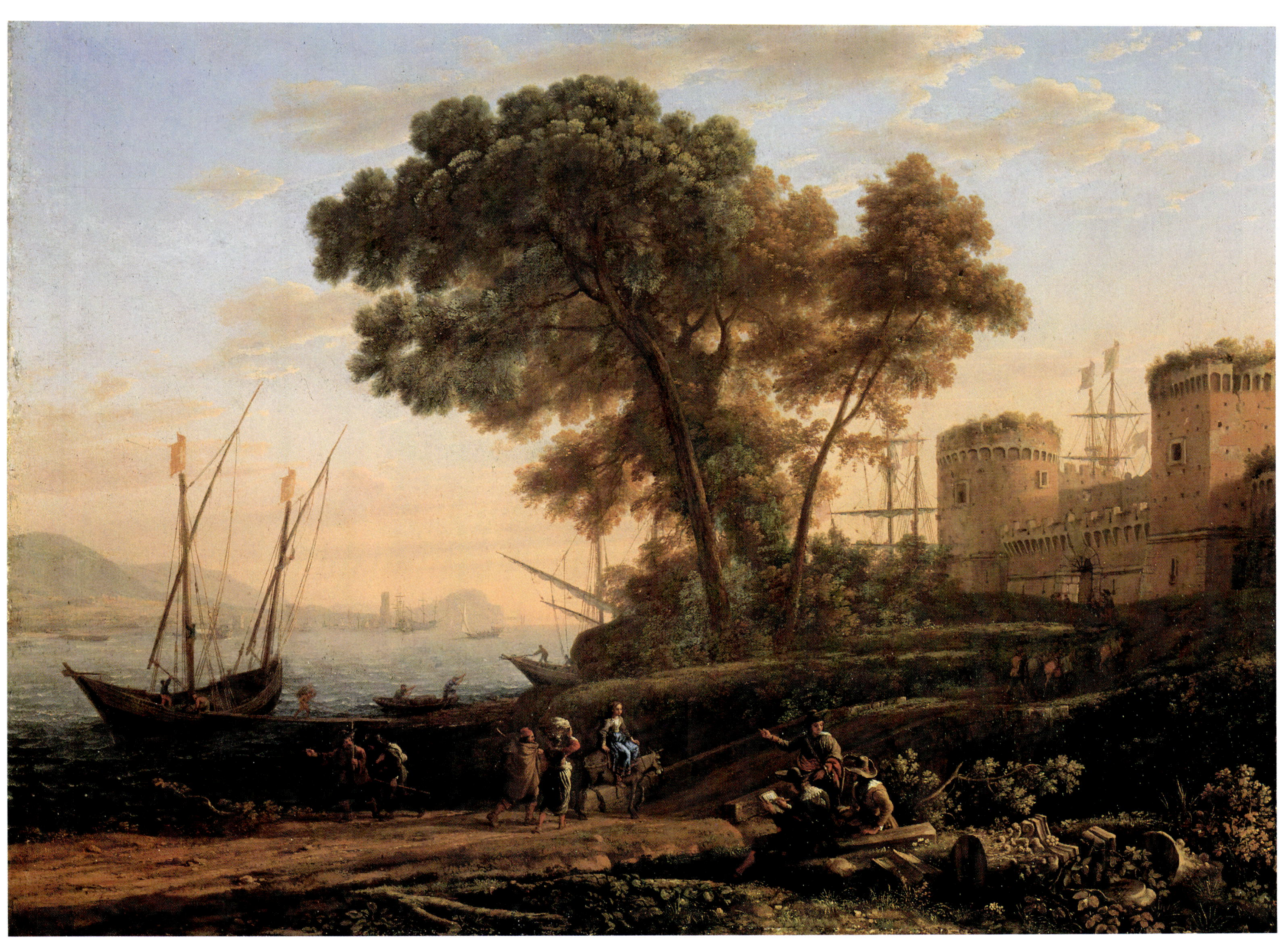

Aert van der Neer

1603/4-1677 • DUTCH

Winter Landscape

c. 1650

LITTLE IS KNOWN ABOUT THE ARTIST, at least when comparing his life with many of his contemporaries in Holland's Golden Age of painting. He worked primarily in Amsterdam, and like many Dutch artists he became a specialist in a particular subject. Unable to make a living at painting, he kept a wineshop from 1658 to 1662.

For Van der Neer, winter scenes were especially appealing. Although the many figures are depicted enjoying sledding, skating, or playing a primitive form of golf, Van der Neer successfully transferred to the viewer the biting cold of a winter's day pressing on this country town in Holland. The frozen canal is Van der Neer's central theme, just as the canal was the center of the village's economic and social life.

Oil on canvas, 23 x 27½"
Gift of Audrey Emery, 1953

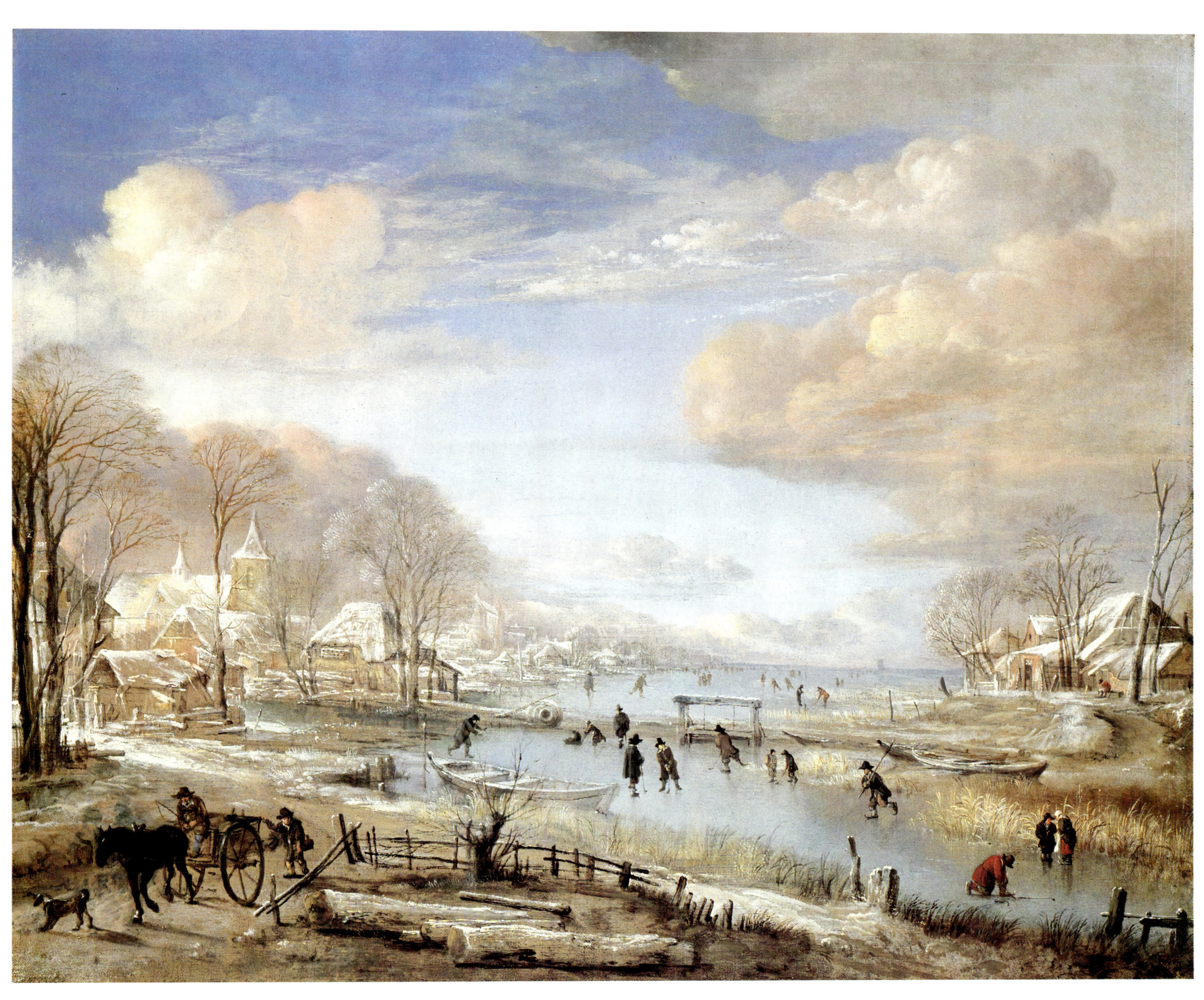

Gerard ter Borch

1617-1681 • DUTCH

A Music Party

c. 1675

TER BORCH, JAN STEEN, AND PIETER DE HOOCH were called the "Little Dutchmen," not in any deprecating sense but because they specialized in subject matter that was intimate and personal. Their paintings were concerned primarily with everyday events and unpretentious people working or playing.

Ter Borch was well traveled, journeying to Italy, Spain, Germany, and England after studies with his father. It is thought that he was deeply impressed with Velázquez's painting, although it is difficult to see the Spanish master's influence directly. Being so cosmopolitan, Ter Borch was attracted to subjects of charm and grace, such as the *Music Party*. He was a master of this type of genre painting, the interior scene with two or three gallants and frequently an elegantly gowned lady. Probably no other artist exceeded Ter Borch's ability to paint illusionistically, so that the fabrics, their texture and sheen, and the play of light over musicians and furniture are rendered as convincingly as possible and frozen in time.

Oil on wood panel, 22⅞ x 18⅝"
Bequest of Mary M. Emery, 1927

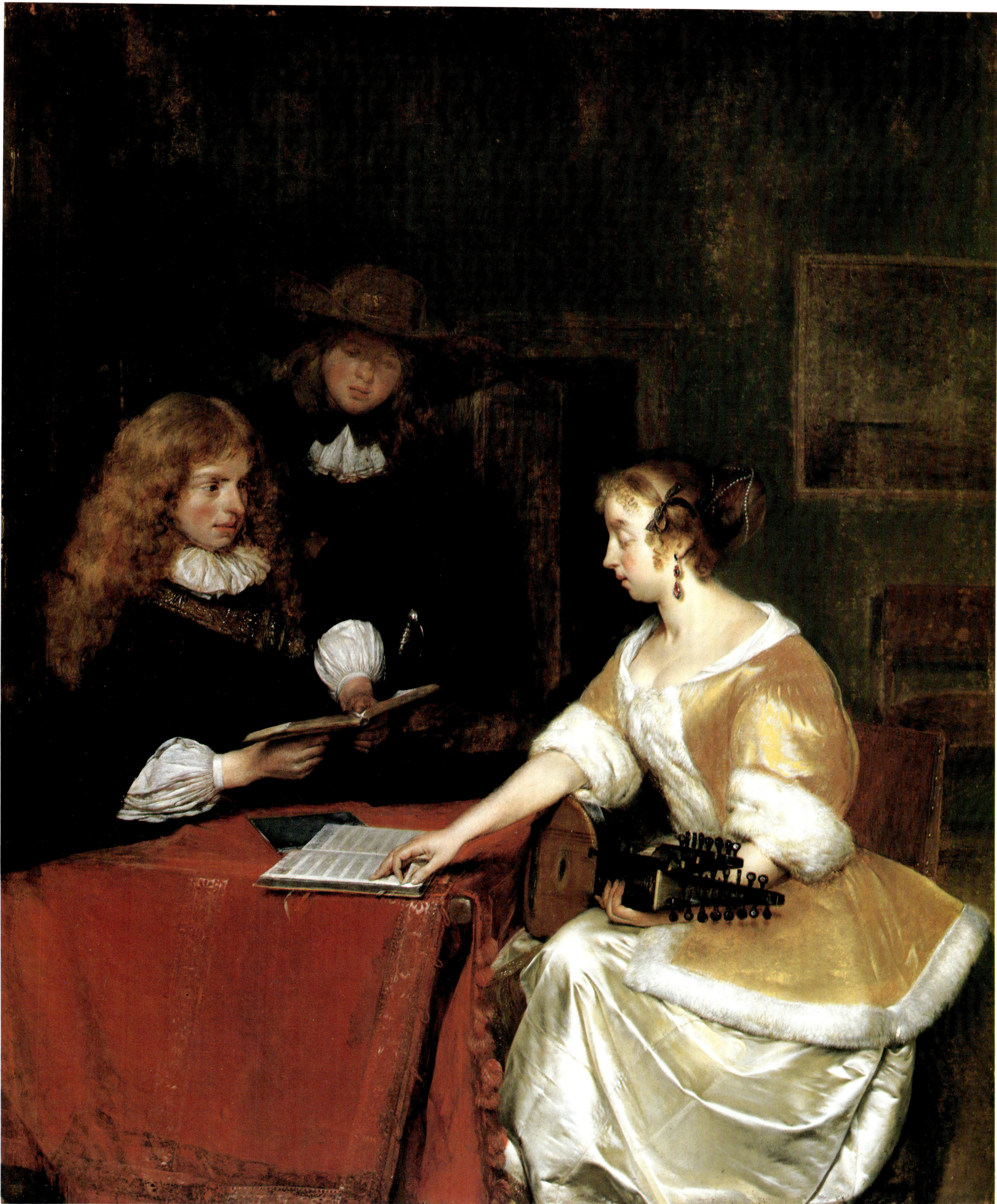

Bartolomé Esteban Murillo

1617-1682 • SPANISH

St. Thomas of Villanueva Dividing His Clothes Among Beggar Boys

1664-1667

IN THE NINETEENTH CENTURY, world opinion regarded Murillo as the greatest painter Spain had ever produced. Today, he is certainly ranked among that country's leading artists, one of three or four of the most important painters in the seventeenth century, Spain's artistic Golden Age. Murillo worked principally in Seville, where he founded the Academy for artists, and his fame and talent led him to become court painter to King Charles II of Spain and to numerous commissions from churches and convents.

In 1664, Murillo signed a contract with the monastery of San Agustín in Seville to paint the *retablo mayor*, a principal altarpiece, with scenes illustrating the life of Thomas of Villanueva, an Augustinian saint noted for his generosity and charity. It is not known how many paintings were incorporated originally into the *retablo*, an elaborate grouping of paintings in a carved and gilded framework of imposing dimensions, but at least four exist today.

The Cincinnati painting depicts an event in the childhood of the saint, the distribution of his own clothes to needy children, representing the compassionate, charitable works for which Thomas of Villanueva was venerated. Murillo's tender rendering in richly applied earth colors and softened forms (a manner the Spanish call *estilo vaporoso*) transcends the religious intention the painting once had in a church.

Oil on canvas, 86½ x 58¾″
Bequest of Mary M. Emery, 1927

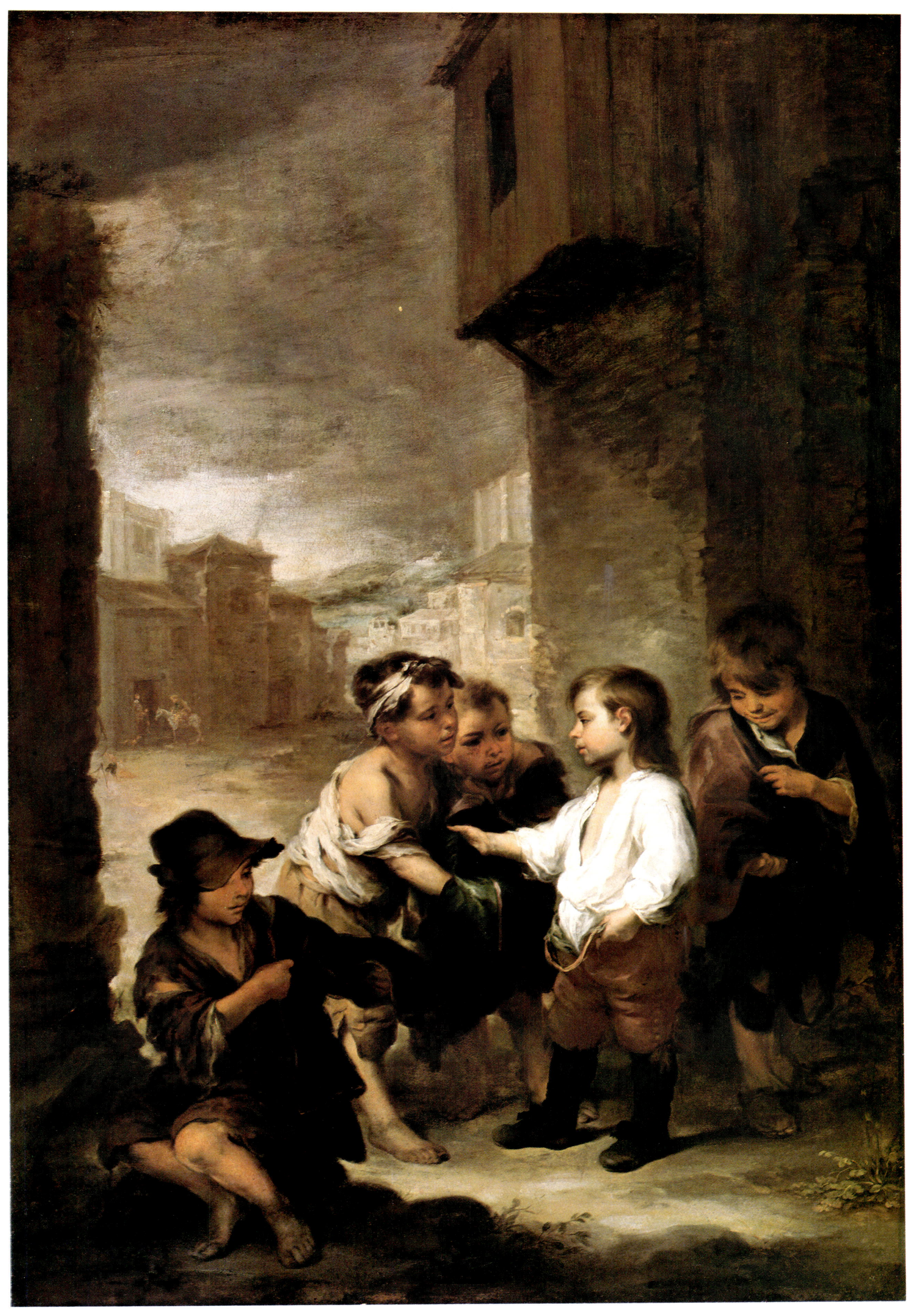

Jacob van Ruisdael

1629-1682 • DUTCH

Scene in Westphalia with Castle of Bentheim

AFTER 1650

THIS LANDSCAPE IS FROM RUISDAEL'S later years, an improvisation that included the Castle of Bentheim, still in existence today, located on the Dutch-German border in Westphalia. Nearly thirty paintings of this subject were done by Ruisdael, who apparently first visited the site in 1650.

Ruisdael entered the Haarlem painters' guild in 1648 after studying with his father and uncle, Salomon van Ruisdael. In eastern Holland and western Germany, Jacob saw his first mountains, and his paintings thereafter gave special attention to this topographical element so unlike the flat Dutch landscape and the low horizon lines frequently seen in Dutch painting. Ruisdael is recognized as the most important realist landscape painter of the seventeenth century in the Netherlands. He exerted tremendous influence on a number of painters, primarily Meindert Hobbema.

Oil on canvas, 40¼ x 49⅝"
Gift of Mary Hanna, 1946

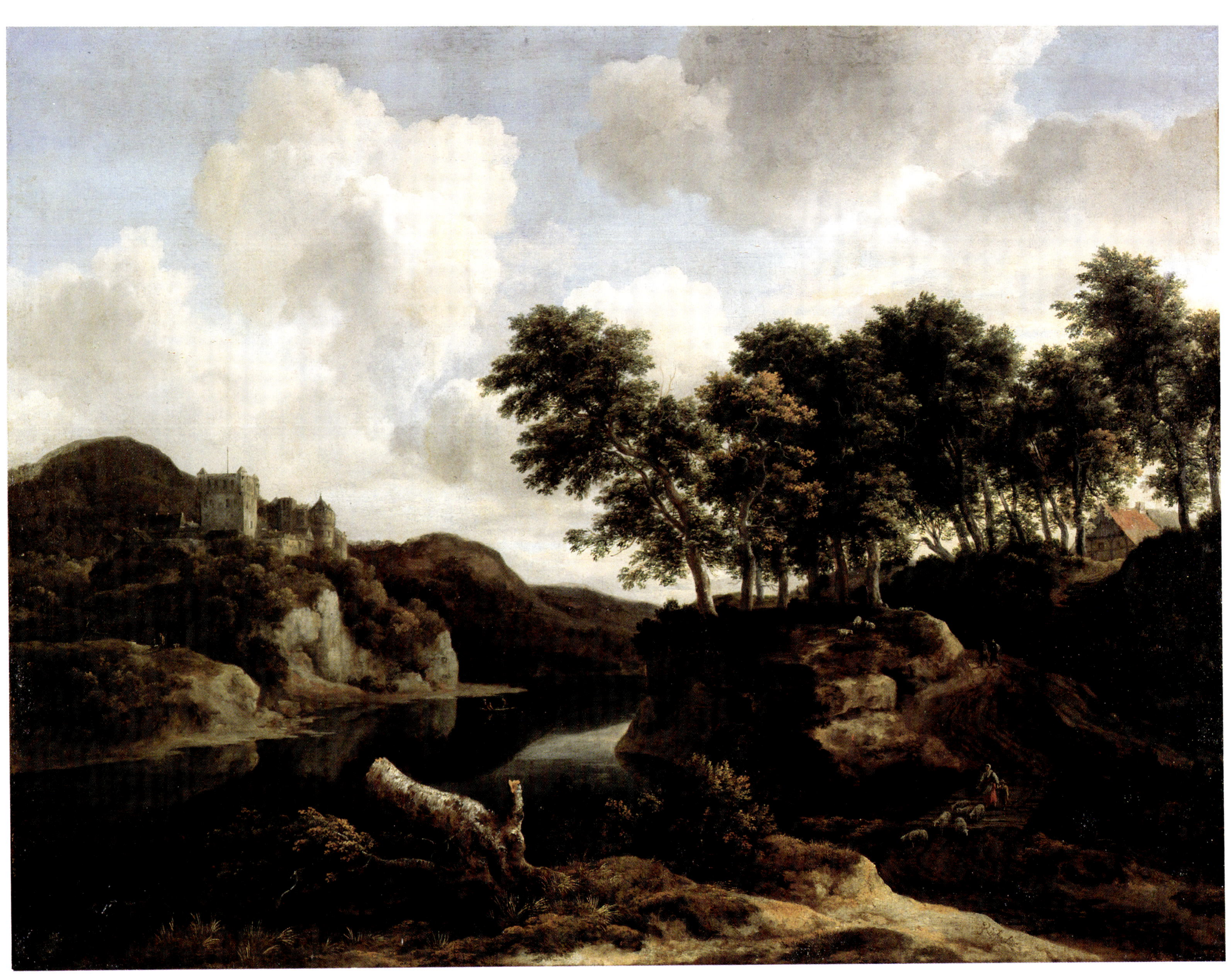

Giovanni Battista Tiepolo

1696-1770 • ITALIAN

San Carlos Borromeo

1767-1769

TIEPOLO WAS VENICE'S last artist of greatness. He was born and trained in that magical city of canals on the Adriatic, where he worked in many churches and palaces not only in oils but also in fresco. By age nineteen he was an accomplished artist. Called to Würzburg in 1750 to decorate the palace of the prince-bishops, he enlisted his talented sons to assist him there and later in Spain where he went at the request of King Charles III in 1762. Continuing the pattern set by another Venetian, Titian, who journeyed to the court of the Holy Roman emperor and Spanish king, Charles V, Tiepolo went to decorate rooms in the Royal Palace at Madrid. He died in that capital city.

Not far from Madrid, the town of Aranjuez was favored by Spanish monarchs. There they built a royal palace with some of the loveliest gardens in Spain. By order of King Charles III, the monastery of San Pascual Bailón was built there between 1765 and 1770, its altars to be decorated with paintings by Tiepolo. About 1767 a series of seven paintings was begun, with installation intended for the church by 1769. In this fragmentary painting from the series, Tiepolo depicted the saint Charles Borromeo (who died in 1584) worshiping before the crucified Jesus, symbolic of the saint's prayer for relief from the plague that wracked Milan in the sixteenth century. The animosity between Tiepolo and the priest in charge of the church may have caused rejection of the paintings, for by 1787 works of other, inferior artists replaced the masterpieces by Tiepolo. The final efforts of the Venetian painter were consigned to storage and near destruction. Today, the Cincinnati painting remains a fragment of a once-grand altarpiece of imposing size.

The last glories of Venetian painting are seen in the sure brushwork and creamy colors that characterize Tiepolo's virtuoso style. He was essentially a Rococo artist, given to lighter, pastel colors and angular, lively rhythms in his compositions. As painter, etcher, and master of drawing, Tiepolo was the spectacular finale to the great Venetian tradition of Titian, Tintoretto, and Veronese.

Oil on canvas, 48¼ x 43⅞"
J. J. Emery Endowment, 1924

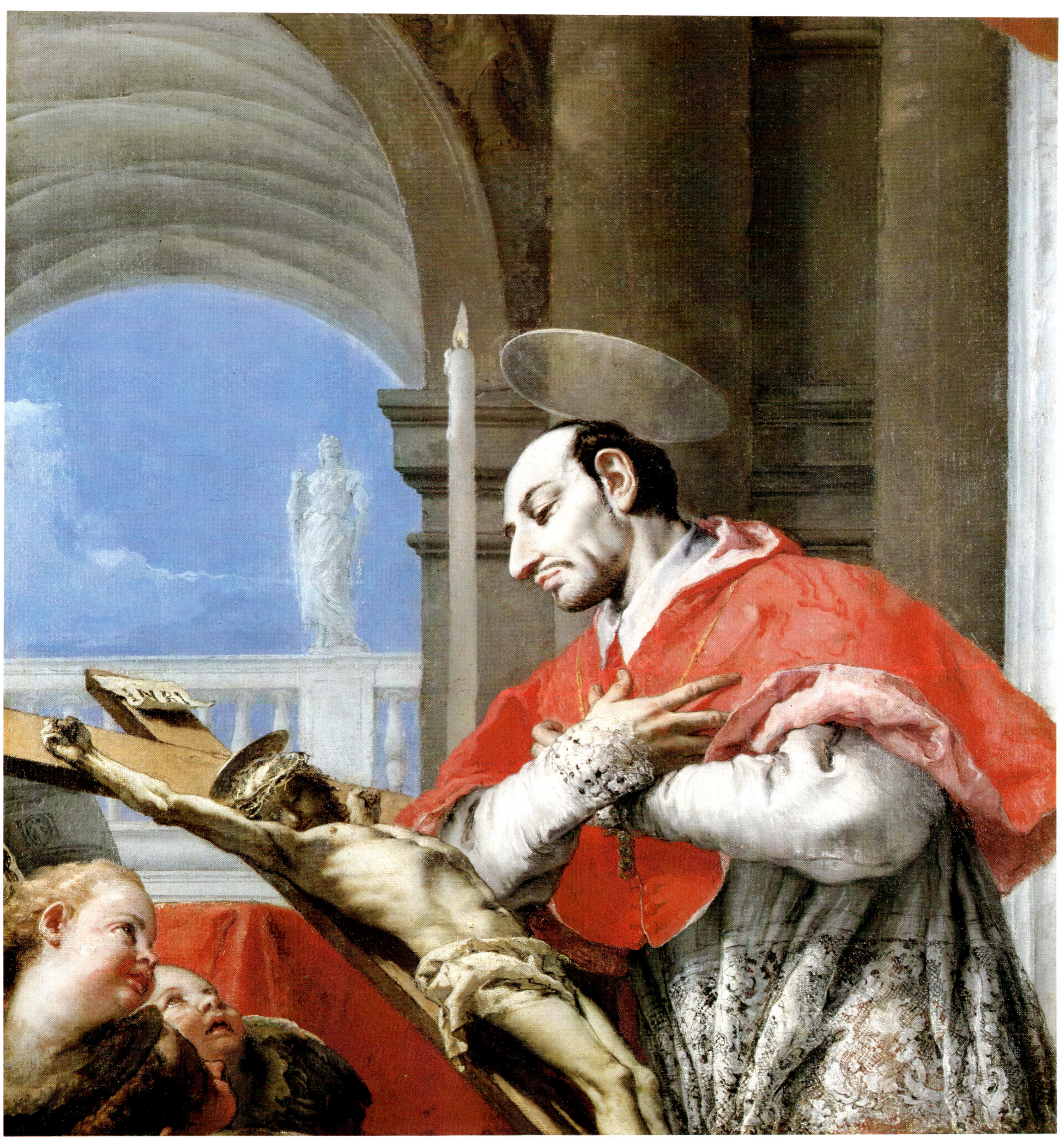

Canaletto

(GIOVANNI ANTONIO CANAL) 1697-1768 • ITALIAN

The Arch of Septimius Severus in Rome

c. 1743

CANALETTO WAS BORN IN VENICE, studied there with his artist-father, and developed a style sensitive to light and shade, subdued coloring, and precise drawing. He was immensely popular for the landscapes he painted, called *vedute*; so much so that many of his subjects were repeated by him and copied by others.

Canaletto's paintings usually record quite accurately the appearance of the architectural monuments he knew and loved in Venice, Rome, and England. But he also painted a type of painting called a *cappriccio*, a fantasy-view concocted of actual elements mixed with incorrect spatial relationships or juxtapositions. His art was in demand by aristocrats on the Grand Tour, and even King George III of England was an important collector of his works. While Canaletto's paintings, prints, and drawings were not collected necessarily as souvenirs of visits, his works were impressive, beautiful "landscapes of recollection."

Canaletto, already an accomplished painter, made at least one visit to Rome about 1720, and there he made many drawings that would serve him well in later years. His finished paintings, like the Cincinnati work, often were developed from sketches and drawings accumulated years earlier. Perspective, light, and shade could all be derived from drawings or engravings with color, details, and figures added. The Arch of Septimius Severus in the Roman Forum (its appearance today is more imposing because of excavation and restoration) was erected in A.D. 203 to commemorate the emperor's victories in the eastern empire. In the background looms the tower of the Capitol and to the right the domed church of Sts. Martin and Luke.

Oil on canvas, 20 1/16 x 27 1/4"
Moch Bequest Purchase Fund, 1926

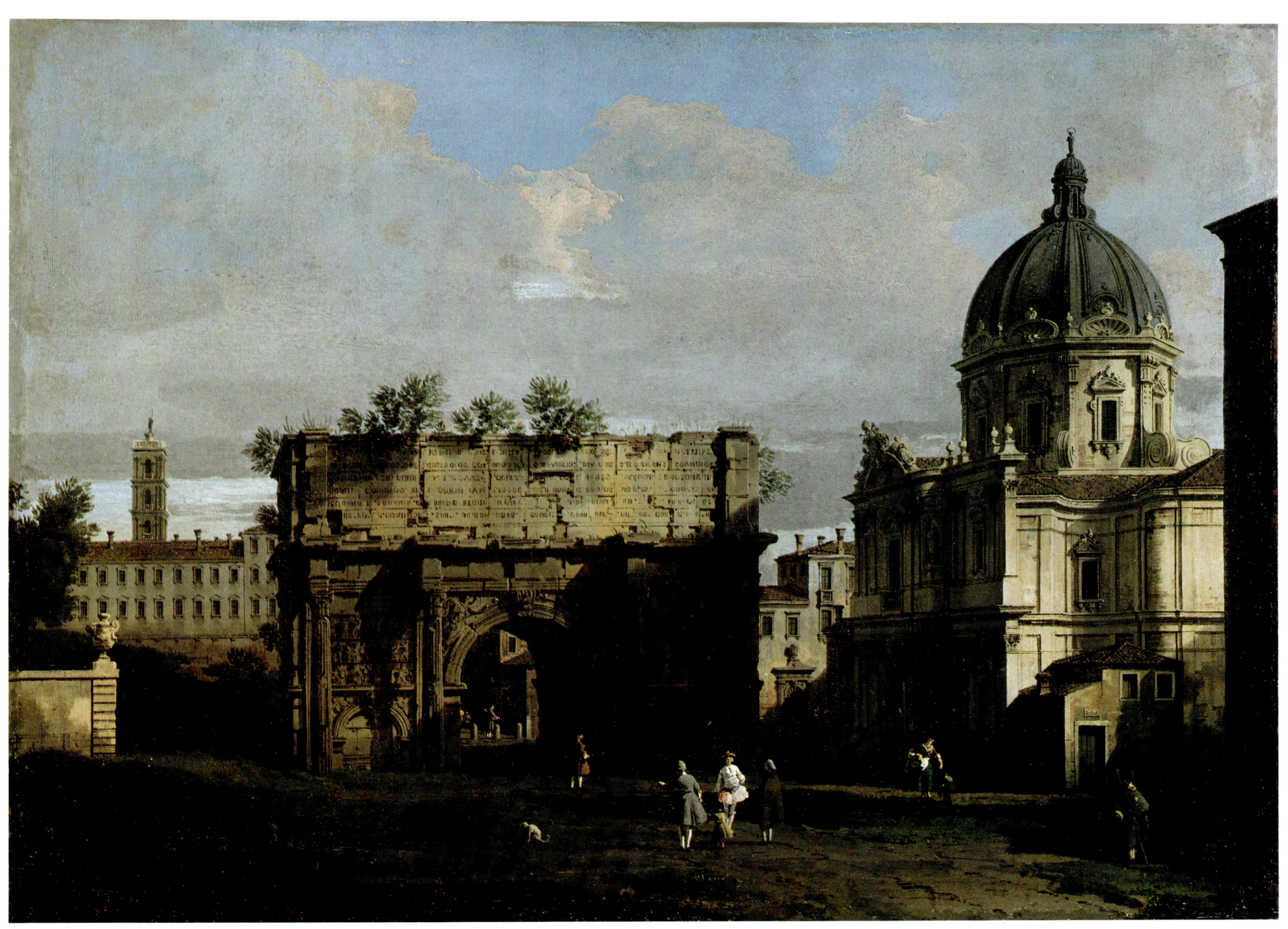

François Boucher

1703-1770 • FRENCH

The Washerwoman

c. 1764

BOUCHER PAINTED THE LIGHT-HEARTED, frivolous France he knew and often imagined before the Revolution destroyed most of the patronage and the world he loved. He was a versatile painter who could execute equally well designs for tapestries, paintings of mythological or pastoral scenes to decorate boudoirs, and portraits of aristocrats. As the protégé of Madame de Pompadour he enjoyed special privileges with the court of Louis XV, and is the supreme French painter of the Rococo period.

Marvelously contrived, Boucher's *The Washerwoman* is a made-up composition of shepherd and flock, crumbling building, mossy shore and pond, and a peasant woman with her laundry that the artist may have observed in the countryside. It depicts a rustic world where men and women act out parts in an attractive setting, much akin to Marie Antoinette's rôle-playing of milk-maid at Versailles as a diversion to stuffy, formal court etiquette. The painting is pure decoration, without intending to intrude itself too strongly into an eighteenth-century French salon where it probably was hung originally.

Oil on canvas, 25 x 32⅝"
Gift of Mary Hanna, 1935

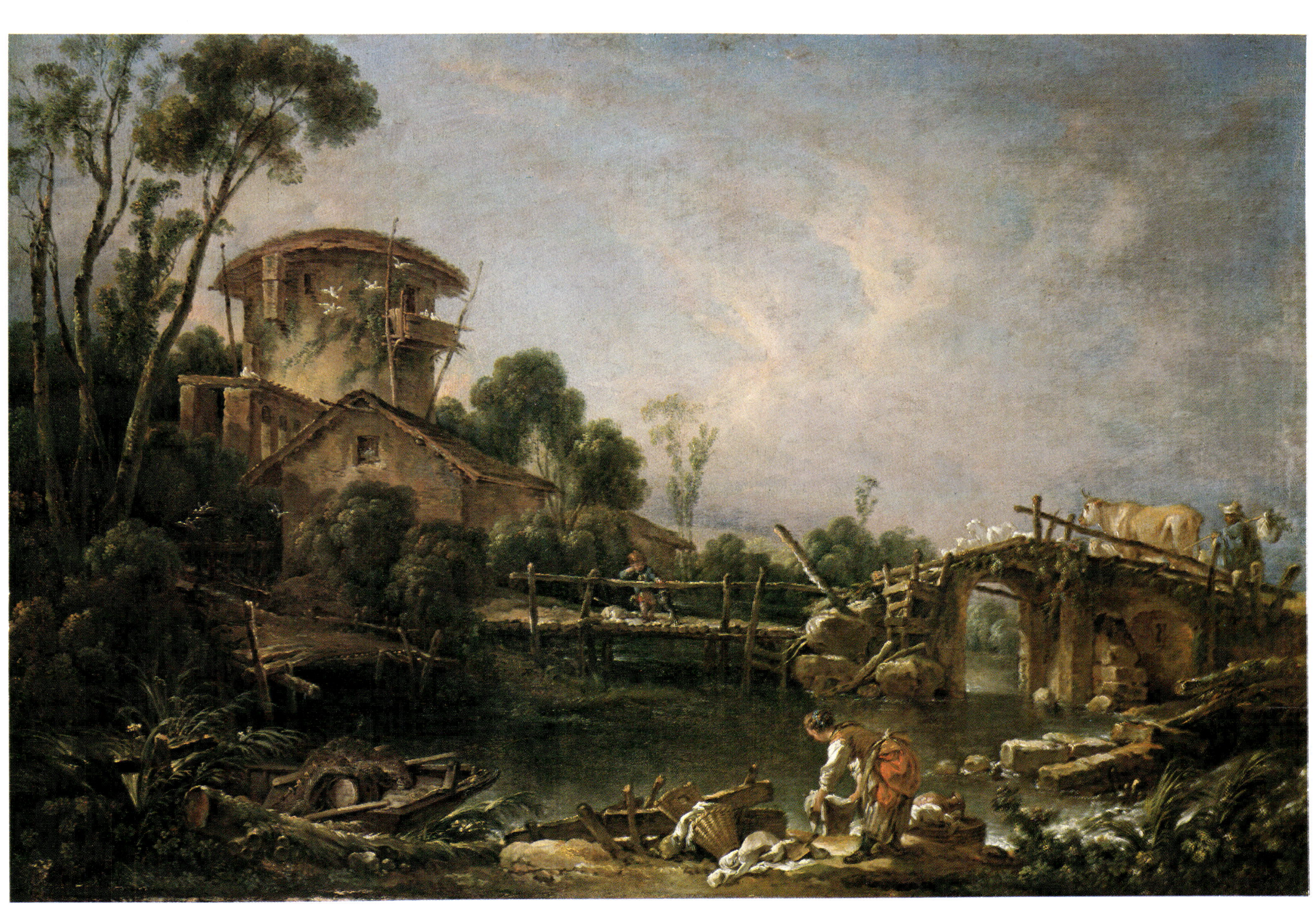

Thomas Gainsborough

1727-1788 • BRITISH

Mrs. Philip Thicknesse

1760

"I'M SICK OF PORTRAITS and wish very much to take my viol da gamba and walk off to some sweet village where I can paint landskips and enjoy the fag end of life in quietness and ease," wrote Gainsborough to a friend. This suggests much about the great British artist. Portrait painting was the livelihood for most British artists in the eighteenth century, no matter what their personal inclination may have been. Landscape painting for Gainsborough, like his passion for music, gave him much pleasure but little pay.

Gainsborough's move from Ipswich to Bath in 1759, the center for society where fashionable aristocrats elegantly paraded and went to see and be seen, placed him where the sitters were who could commission portraits. His brushwork and colors were vivacious and truly Rococo in spirit, appealing to his new clientele. There in 1760 he painted Ann Ford (1737-1824) who two years later would marry Philip Thicknesse, Gainsborough's biographer and early promoter at Ipswich.

Mrs. Thicknesse sat nonchalantly for her portrait, clutching her English guitar (or cittern) and with a bass viol (perhaps Gainsborough's own) hanging in the background. It was informal, even slightly indecorous to be painted in this pose then, but Ann Ford was not the usual sitter. She was charming, daring, and very accomplished as a musician, giving recitals as a singer and performing on the viol da gamba and musical glasses. Gainsborough's portrait is a dashing example of brushwork, imposing in scale and concept, but expressive, too, of a special kinship that existed between two people who loved music.

Oil on canvas, 77⅝ x 53⅛"
Bequest of Mary M. Emery, 1927

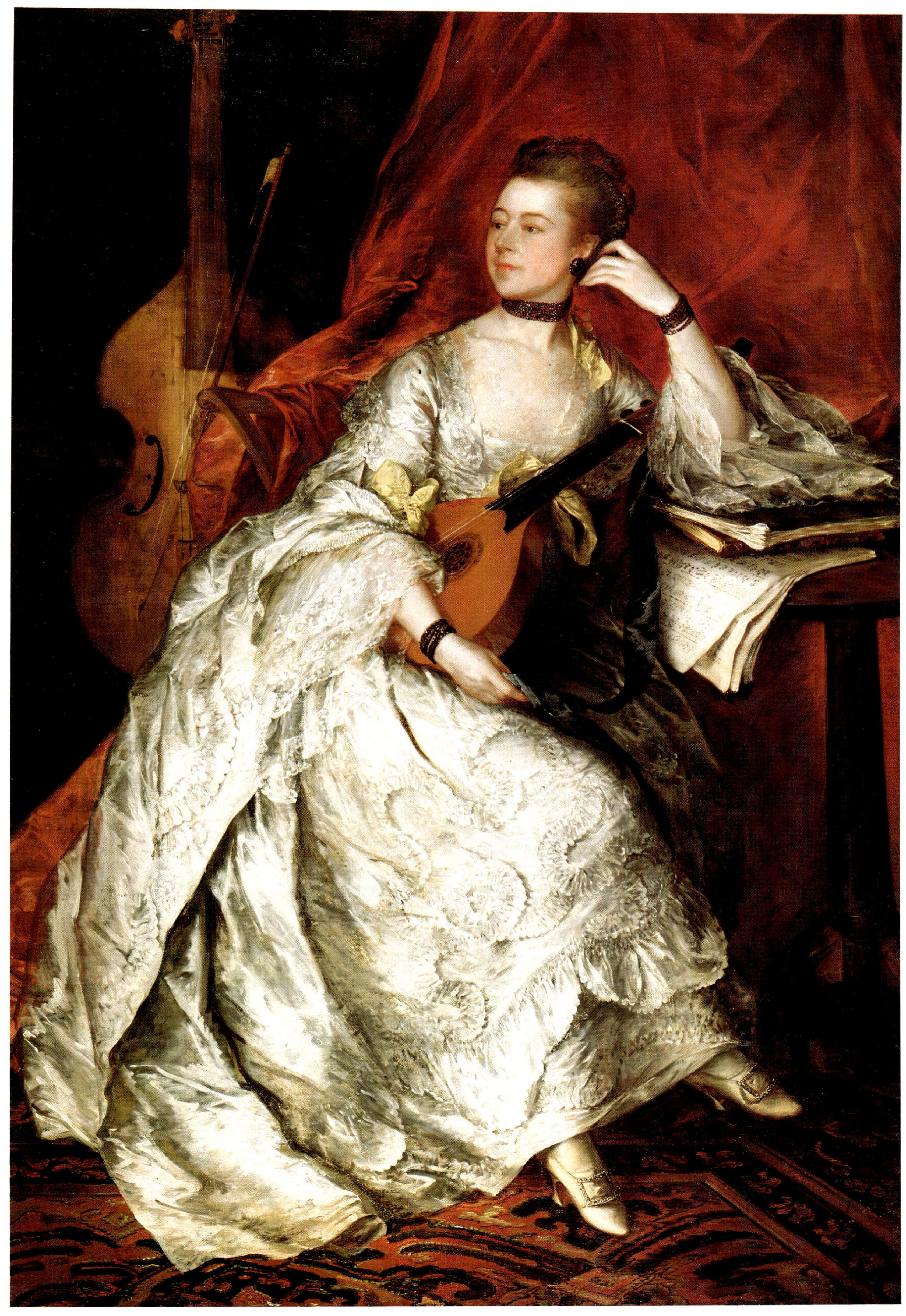

Thomas Gainsborough

1727-1788 • BRITISH

The Cottage Door

c. 1780

PROBABLY THE MOST TELLING comments on Gainsborough as artist and man came from his only true rival, Sir Joshua Reynolds, who devoted one of his learned *Discourses* (the fourteenth) to him and observed: "If ever this nation should produce genius sufficient to acquire to us the honorable distinction of an English School, the name of Gainsborough will be transmitted to posterity, in the history of the art, among the very first of that rising name." As in Gainsborough's own day, it is difficult to assess in what field of specialization he excelled—portraiture, landscapes, or what were then called "fancy pictures." His livelihood depended on portrait commissions, of course, and perhaps no more important English portraitist ever lived. He is among the world's foremost three or four painters of portraits.

Gainsborough's true teacher was nature itself, for he seemed undaunted by the French and Italian influences he knew existed, preferring instead a very individual, instinctive vision of texture, shadows, and impression that his landscape subject suggested to him. Because he did not try to imitate nature to capture a photographically exact likeness of the scene (in fact he disliked the "raw" English topography), his landscapes are often thought to be unfinished, sketchy. A landscape like *The Cottage Door* was based on sketches or preparatory drawings (the drawing for the Cincinnati painting is in the collection of the Duchess of Kent, Coppins, England), but the lyrical interpretation on canvas was the product of his mind's eye.

The Cottage Door combines elements of his "fancy pictures" that incorporated ordinary peasants and children in a lush rural setting incomparably English in appearance and effect. While joy and contentment prevail, the drudgery and hard life of the farm family are only suggested by the figure trudging with a load of wood. Throughout the picture, but especially in areas like the strokes of golden light near the figure at far left, Gainsborough's brushwork is bold, luscious, and vigorous. Painted about 1780 in London where he settled after years at the resort-spa of Bath, this painting employs a theme he used more than once (another version is in the Huntington Library and Art Gallery, San Marino, California).

Oil on canvas, 48¼ x 58¾"

Given in honor of Mr. and Mrs. Charles F. Williams by their children, 1948

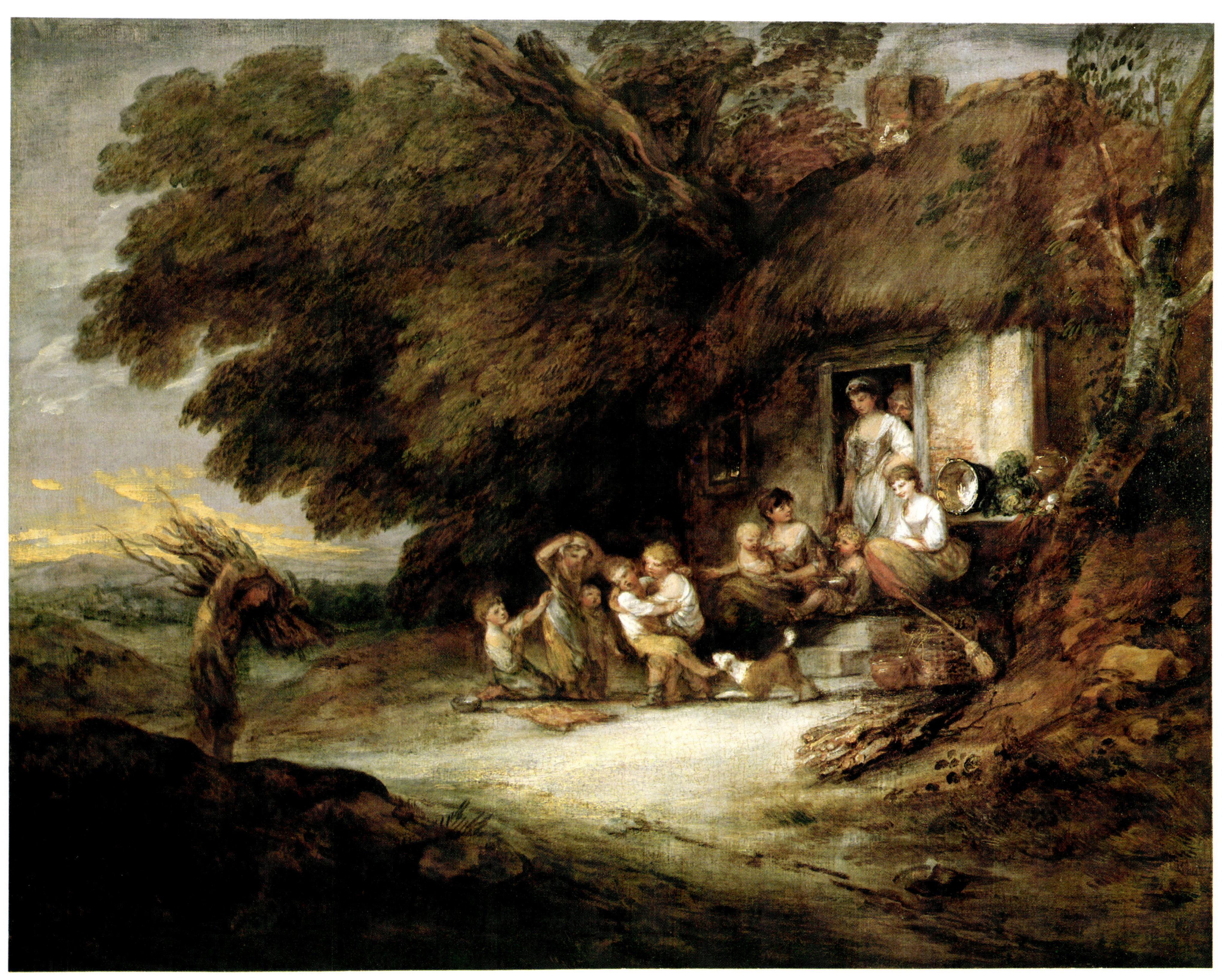

Jean-Honoré Fragonard

1732-1806 • FRENCH

The Letter

c. 1776

FRAGONARD STUDIED FIRST with Chardin and then with Boucher, with whom he remained until 1752 when he won the Prix de Rome. His early reputation rested on his paintings of historical and religious subjects. After studying in Italy from 1756 to 1761, he was widely praised by a growing number of patrons, including Mme. du Barry and courtiers of the Rococo world of France that tumbled with the Revolution. Out of step with the new society and the austere neoclassicism that replaced his world of elegance and femininity, Fragonard died neglected and forgotten. He ranks with the greatest painters of the eighteenth century.

The model in this painting may be one of the Colombe sisters, Marie-Catherine or Adeline Riggieri, actresses at the Comédie Italienne. About 1776, Fragonard painted several portraits of young women reading books or letters, expressing joy, sadness, or pensiveness. Fragonard boasted of his ability to paint a portrait quickly—"in half an hour," he inscribed on the back of one—and this painting has a sketchlike, unfinished quality.

Oil on canvas, 15 x 11⅝"
Gift of Mary Hanna, 1946

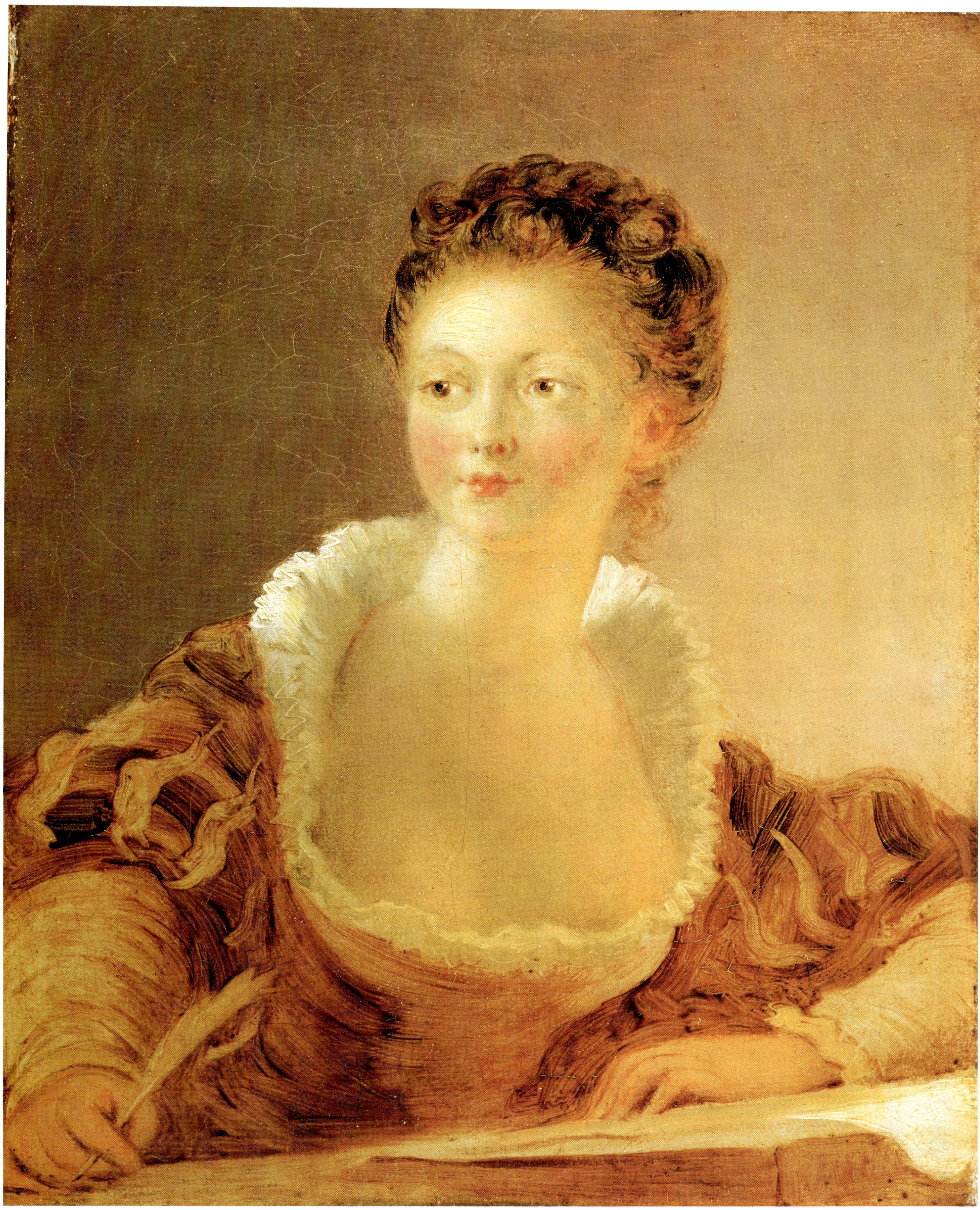

John Singleton Copley

1738-1815 • AMERICAN

Thomas Greene

1758

THE FIRST AMERICAN PAINTER of greatness was John Singleton Copley, who portrayed many of the prosperous men and women of eighteenth-century New England. His portraits were technically accomplished and magnificently posed, boldly colored likenesses that pleased, and provided him with financial security. Copley's life centered in Boston, where he was born. The Revolutionary War reduced commissions as political upheaval diverted the attention of his clients, and Copley left for England in 1774, never to return to the American Colonies.

Exuding self-confidence and with the bearing of the successful businessman he was, Thomas Greene (1705-1763) was painted in 1758, a date noted on the letter held in the Boston merchant's hand. Twice married, his second wife Martha also posed for her portrait by Copley. The ship in full sail probably referred to Greene's commercial interests and adds another focus in the painting some distance beyond the richly covered table. The clutter at his elbow, the sparkle of the knee-buckle, and even the homely touch of wig powder lightly dusting the sitter's shoulder are details of special charm. The pose and setting obviously were derived from English prototype portraits Copley knew from engravings, but the young Copley (only twenty when he painted this stunning portrait) surely was aware of the charming but primitive work of the slightly older artists, John Smibert and Robert Feke.

Oil on canvas, 49½ x 39½"
Gift of Mrs. Carlos A. Hepp, 1958

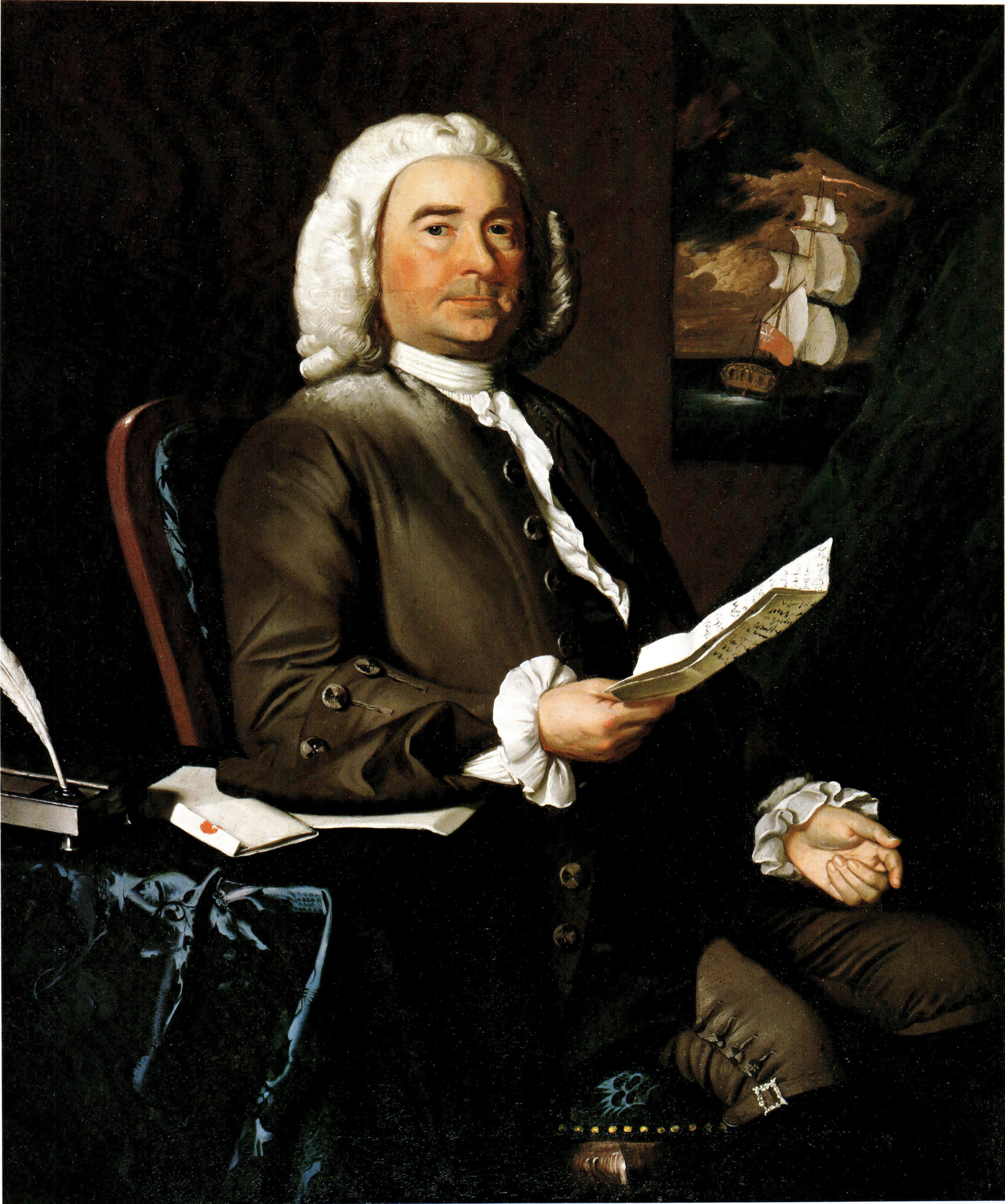

Sir Henry Raeburn

1756-1823 • BRITISH

The Elphinston Children

c. 1812

RAEBURN FLOURISHED as portrait painter in Scotland, but his fame and talent were recognized throughout Britain in a career heaped with honors. His beginnings were humble enough, starting as a goldsmith's apprentice at age fifteen, but graduating to portrait miniature painting and sporadic instruction in art after 1775. By 1787, and after contact with the preeminent portraitist of his day, Sir Joshua Reynolds, he was settled in Edinburgh where he remained the leading Scottish artist of his time.

Edinburgh was a city of Scottish aristocrats, eminent lawyers, and literary figures in the years coinciding with Raeburn's establishment as the Scottish capital city's leading painter. The gentry provided endless commissions. His portraits have a vitality and masculine vigor often lacking in English contemporary portraiture. The identity of the children in the Cincinnati portrait, posed with doll, tambourine, and staff, is not certain, as spellings of the name varied (sometimes Elphinstone), but it is likely that the three children are Alexander Elphinston and his two sisters, Maria and Jane, all born in Bombay.

Oil on canvas, 78 x 60½″
Bequest of Mary M. Emery, 1927

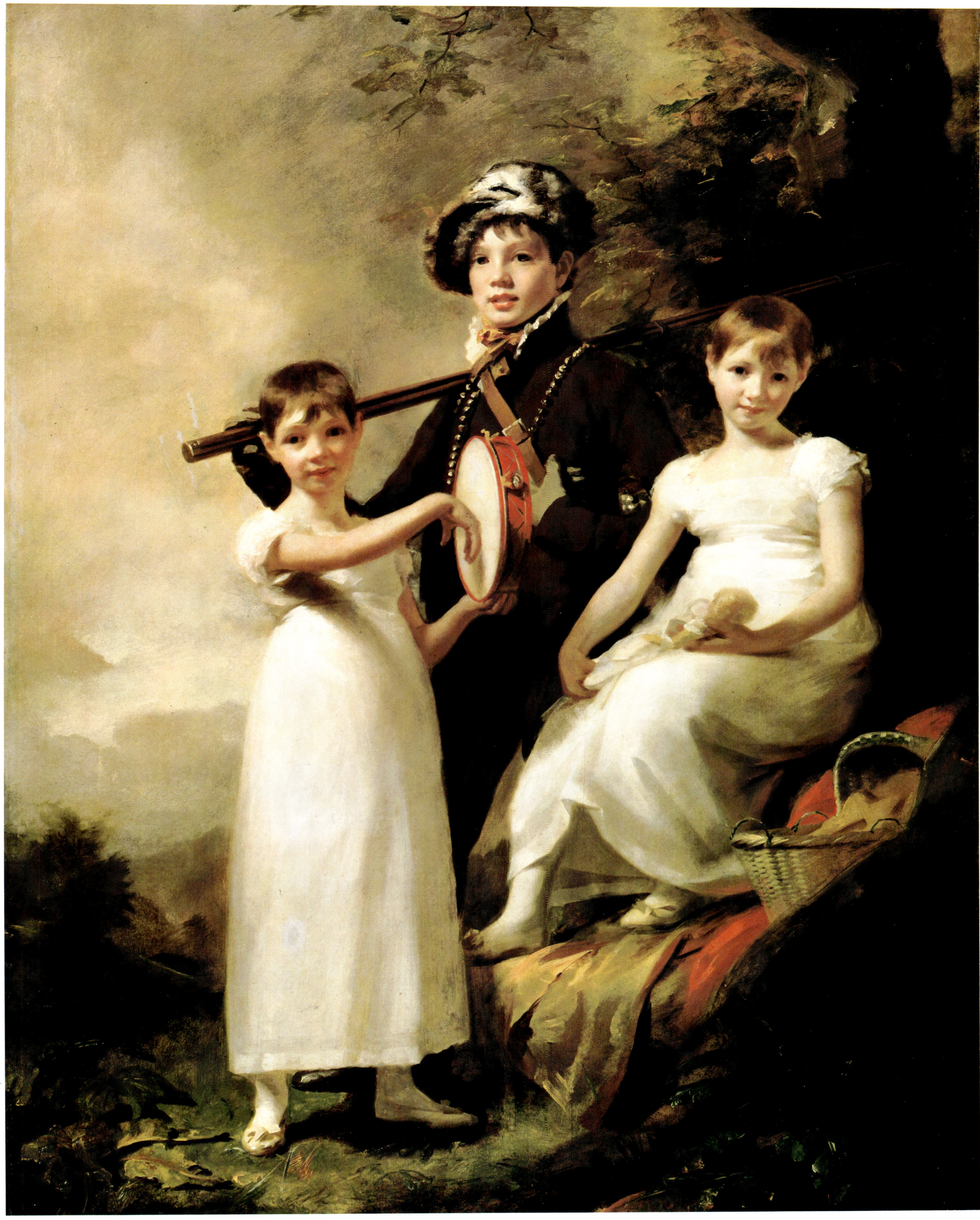

John Trumbull

1756-1843 • AMERICAN

The Sortie from Gibraltar

1788

JOHN TRUMBULL'S TRAINING was typical for many American colonial painters. He journeyed to London and studied with a well-known master where the latest Georgian styles could be seen and where he could learn history painting. In Trumbull's case Benjamin West was his mentor, and he entered West's studio in 1784. Trumbull was equally at home in England and America, painting portraits and making a pictorial record of major events in the Revolutionary War. He lived in England until 1789, served as one of the Jay Treaty commissioners from 1794 to 1804, worked in New York from 1804 to 1808, in London from 1808 to 1816, and served as director of the American Academy of Art thereafter. He returned to New Haven, Connecticut, by 1839, critical of younger artists and resentful of what he regarded as competition.

Trumbull's best works were the small, colorful portraits he did prior to 1804. These portraits have a vital and fresh quality to them, and their style served the artist well in the historical paintings that secured his reputation. While in London in 1787, he heard the story of the siege of Gibraltar (then as now a British-held fortress) by the Spanish who had constructed breastworks to support their attack. In a daring move, the British (under General Elliot, shown in the center and raising his hand over the fallen Spanish officer, Don José Barboza) marched out of their fort on November 26, 1781, and destroyed the Spanish guns and emplacements. Trumbull selected the moment of the magnanimous gesture, setting it against the flames and thrill of victory. Each officer in General Elliot's suite may be identified. in Trumbull's dramatic painting that merges history painting and portraiture. Three versions of different sizes are known of this subject. The Cincinnati painting was recorded by Trumbull as a work with "portraits from life, intended for the engraver." Indeed, this very painting served as the model for an engraving by William Sharp.

Oil on canvas, 20 x 30"
J. J. Emery Endowment, 1922

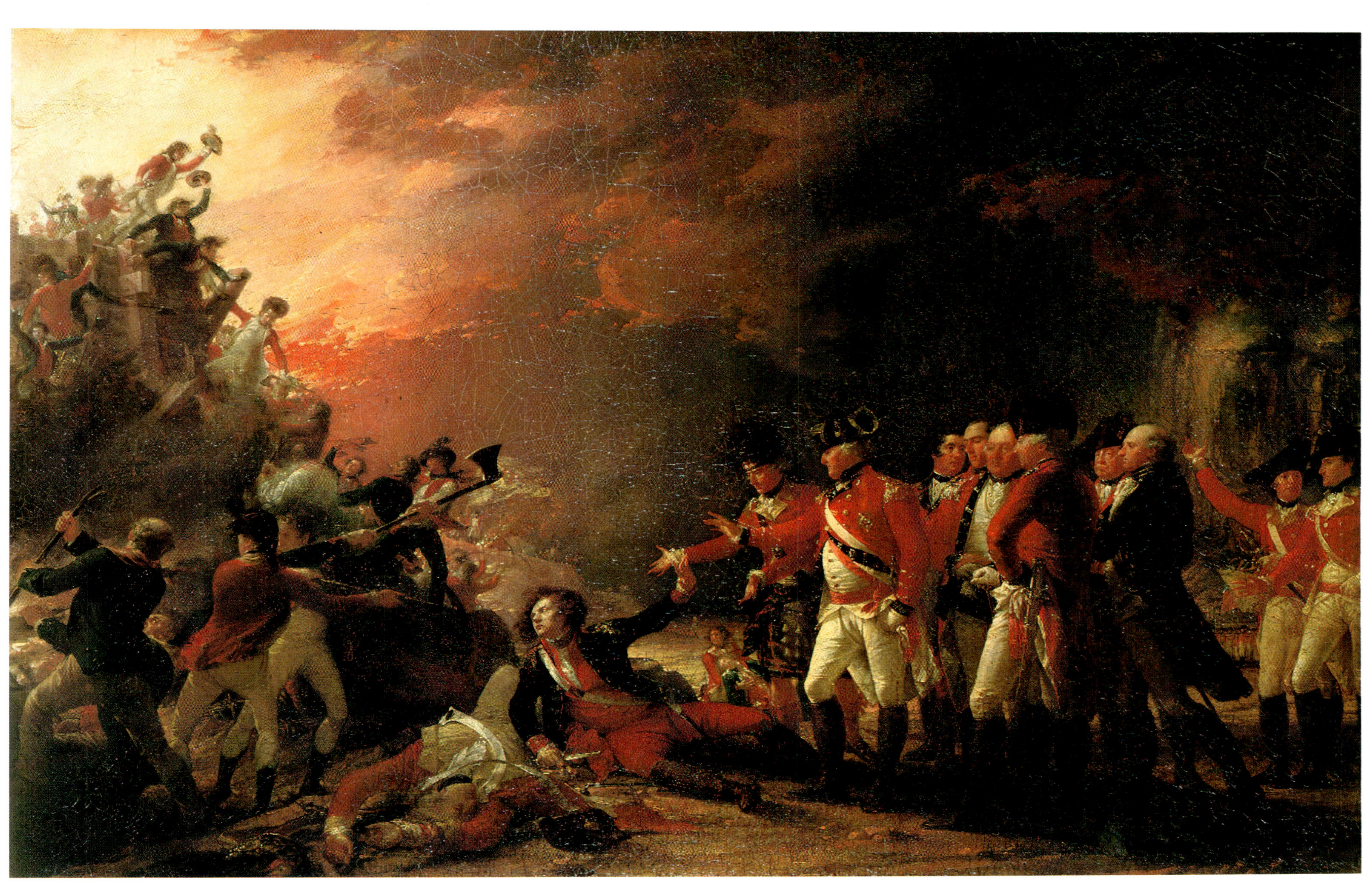

John Constable

1776-1837 • BRITISH

Waterloo Bridge

c. 1824

WATERLOO BRIDGE across the Thames was opened with festivities on June 18, 1817, on the second anniversary of the battle it commemorated. Presumably Constable witnessed the ceremony, as he was in London on that date. From 1819 when Constable first considered this subject until 1832 when he first exhibited a painting of it, he returned to it again and again with fascination and affection.

Constable's panoramic view includes the imposing dome of St. Paul's Cathedral, the houses of Adelphi Terrace at the left, and the Shot Tower at the far right. His horizon line is placed low on the canvas, as the Dutch artists had done in the seventeenth century. Clouds dominate the upper two-thirds of the canvas. Sky and clouds were Constable's abiding interests during his lifetime, and with them in his landscapes he sought an art where "all is subservient to the one object in view, the embodying a pure apprehension of natural effect." The Cincinnati painting may well be the version Constable painted in 1824 and referred to as "a small balloon to be let off as a forerunner of the large one."

Oil on canvas, 21 11/16 x 30 11/16"
Gift of Mary Hanna, 1946

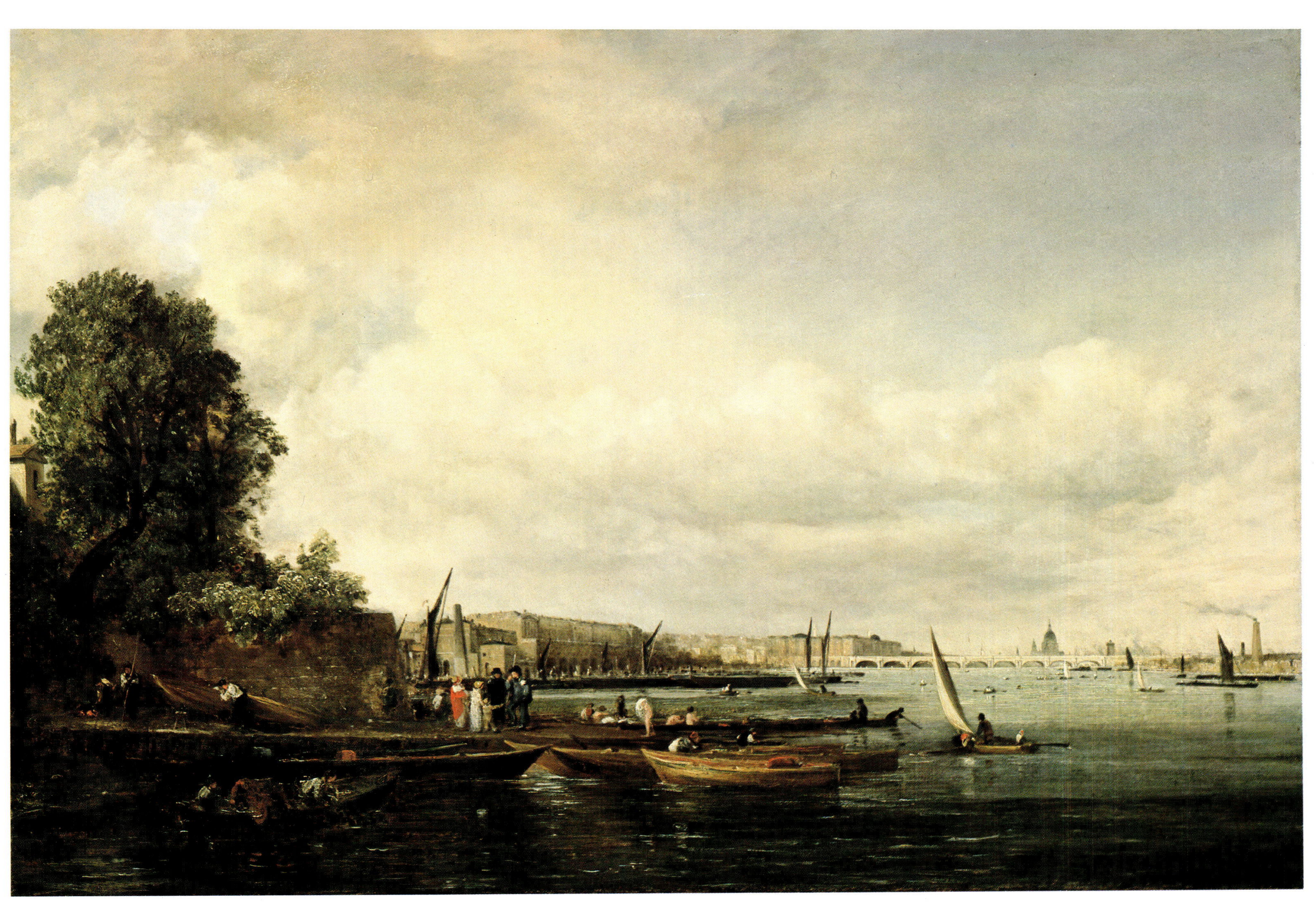

Jean-Auguste-Dominique Ingres

1780-1867 • FRENCH

Portrait of Luigi Cherubini

1841

INGRES WAS AN ASSISTANT in J.-L. David's studio by 1800, and by 1806, with Napoleon in power, he went to Rome to study at the French Academy. Influenced by Renaissance painting, particularly the art of Raphael, Ingres developed an emphasis on line and design that distinguished his work throughout his lifetime. Color for Ingres was minor and always subservient to line. Painting was not the art of coloring a drawing, of tinting and shading. Drawing was Ingres' constant concern, and he was one of the world's foremost *virtuosi* of the pencil portrait, executing hundreds of studies and finished drawings. He persisted in explaining: "To draw does not mean simply to reproduce contours; drawing does not consist merely of line: drawing is also expression, the inner form, the plane, modeling."

Luigi Cherubini (1760-1842) was born in Florence and began his studies there at the age of six with his father. By 1788 he settled in Paris, becoming director of the prestigious Paris Conservatoire from 1821 to 1841. Few composers were as highly esteemed in their lifetimes as Cherubini, and yet today his works are seldom performed. His compositions were models for Beethoven and Schumann. In the Cincinnati portrait, the composer is shown with three of his operatic scores at his elbow. Another version of this portrait, finished a year later, is in the Louvre.

Oil on canvas, 32⅜ x 28″
Bequest of Mary M. Emery, 1927

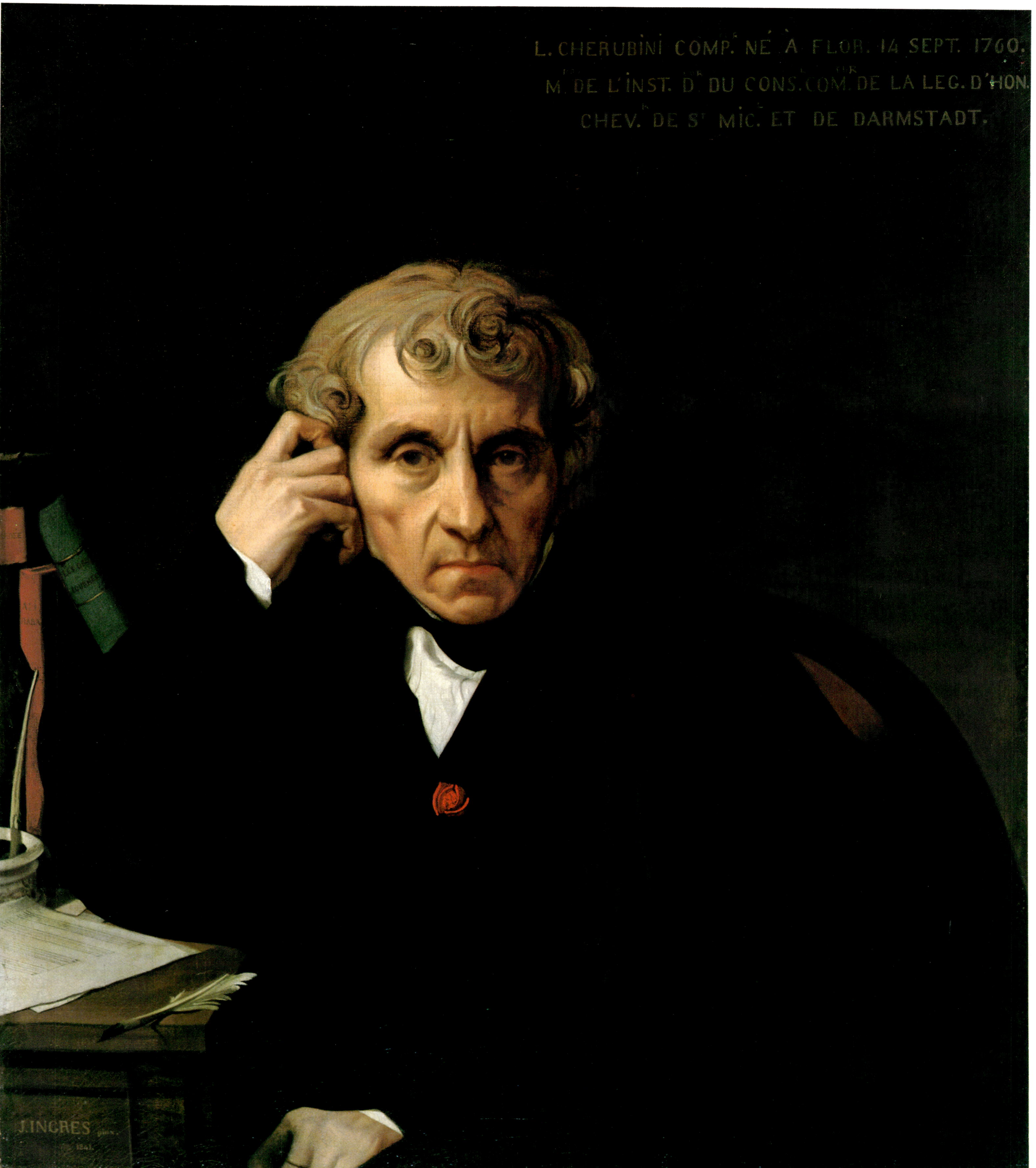
L. CHERUBINI COMP. NÉ À FLOR. 14 SEPT. 1760.
M. DE L'INST. D. DU CONS. COM. DE LA LEG. D'HON.
CHEV. DE S. MIC. ET DE DARMSTADT.
J. INGRES
1841.

Jean-Baptiste-Camille Corot

1796-1875 • FRENCH

The Ruins of the Chateau of Pierrefonds

1830s, 1867

THE LITTLE FRENCH VILLAGE of Barbizon attracted in the early nineteenth century a group of artists dedicated to painting the landscape in the out-of-doors. This was called *plein-air* painting, and, although artists have throughout the centuries sketched and made studies with easels set up under the sky, it was the Barbizon artists who first exploited it to the fullest. They drew on the traditions of English and Dutch landscape painting and held a sensitive appreciation of nature and peasant-laborers. The French artists envisioned a modern life of permanence and peace only if it returned to principles espoused by the philosopher Jean-Jacques Rousseau.

Corot painted out-of-doors near Paris and in the Italian countryside as early as 1825. Returning to France, he worked out-of-doors in warm weather but completed his large paintings indoors in the winter before submitting them to the Salon, the most important showcase in France in the eighteenth and nineteenth centuries. Although he offered no formal teaching to artists, he was the center of a group of painters at Barbizon and was recognized by 1850 as the leading landscape painter in France. He was an inspiration to the Impressionists who admired his direct, fresh approach to painting in the face of Nature.

Pierrefonds, a town in northern France, boasted an impressive castle of the fourteenth or fifteenth century that had fallen into ruins by the nineteenth century when Napoleon III ordered its restoration. When Corot painted its crumbling grandeur, however, it was not yet renovated. Its history forgotten, Corot merged it in a setting of trees, a pond, two figures in a small boat, and a placid sky creating a pastoral scene of poetry and charm, yet dependent for effectiveness on direct observation of the landscape. The broadly painted chateau and background date the canvas in the 1830s, but Corot repainted the foreground in his mature, atmospheric style for entry in the 1867 Salon.

Oil on canvas, 29½ x 42″

Gift of Emilie L. Heine in memory of Mr. and Mrs. John Hauck, 1940

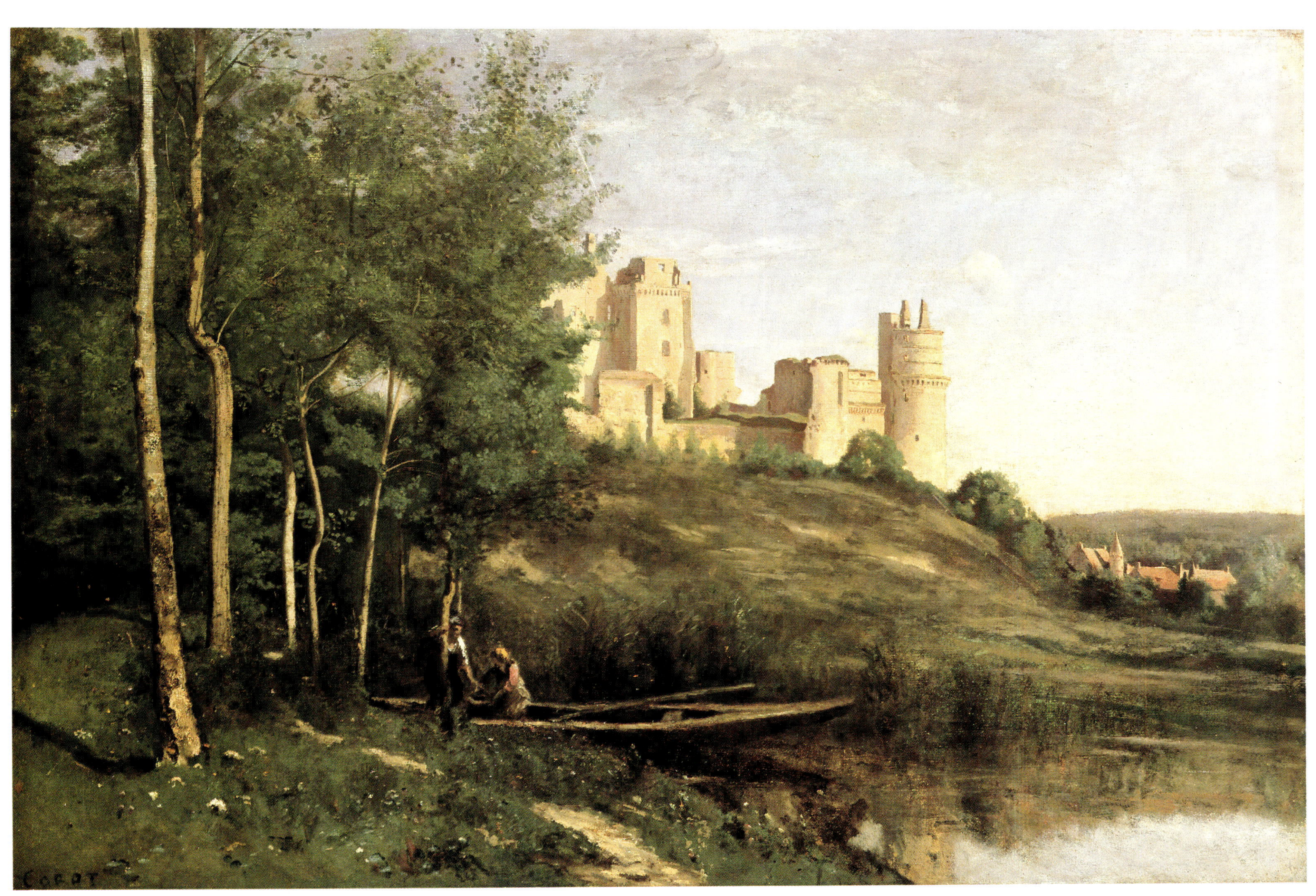
COROT

Thomas Cole

1801-1848 • AMERICAN

View Across Frenchman's Bay from Mt. Desert Island, after a Squall

1845

ONLY IN THE NINETEENTH CENTURY did the landscape become a popular subject for American artists. Their interest paralleled that of the Romantic poets and Transcendentalist writers, men like Thoreau, Emerson, and William Cullen Bryant. The painter, Thomas Cole, wedded an artist's eye for the dramatic untamed wilderness with the intellectual's vision of nature in her poetical, philosophical relationships to man.

Cole was America's preeminent landscape painter before 1850, with a career compressed into a brief span that included European study, numerous sketching trips throughout the many states, and travel in New England and along the Hudson River. A group of talented artists who shared Cole's interest in translating to canvas a sense of all-powerful nature became known as the Hudson River School. They were seeking what Bryant avowed in *Thanatopsis*: "Go forth, under the open sky, and list to Nature's teachings."

Cole was not always a Romantic visionary in his paintings, and frequently he was factual and objective in recording the landscape as it appeared to him. In August, 1844, Cole made a sketching trip to Maine, and there he did sixteen views of Mt. Desert Island in his sketchbook. Back in his studio he developed the finished oil painting now in the Cincinnati Art Museum. This panoramic view prefigures the wide-angle vistas loved by the second-generation Hudson River School artists, Frederick Church and Albert Bierstadt.

Oil on canvas, 38¼ x 62½"
Gift of Alice Scarborough, 1925

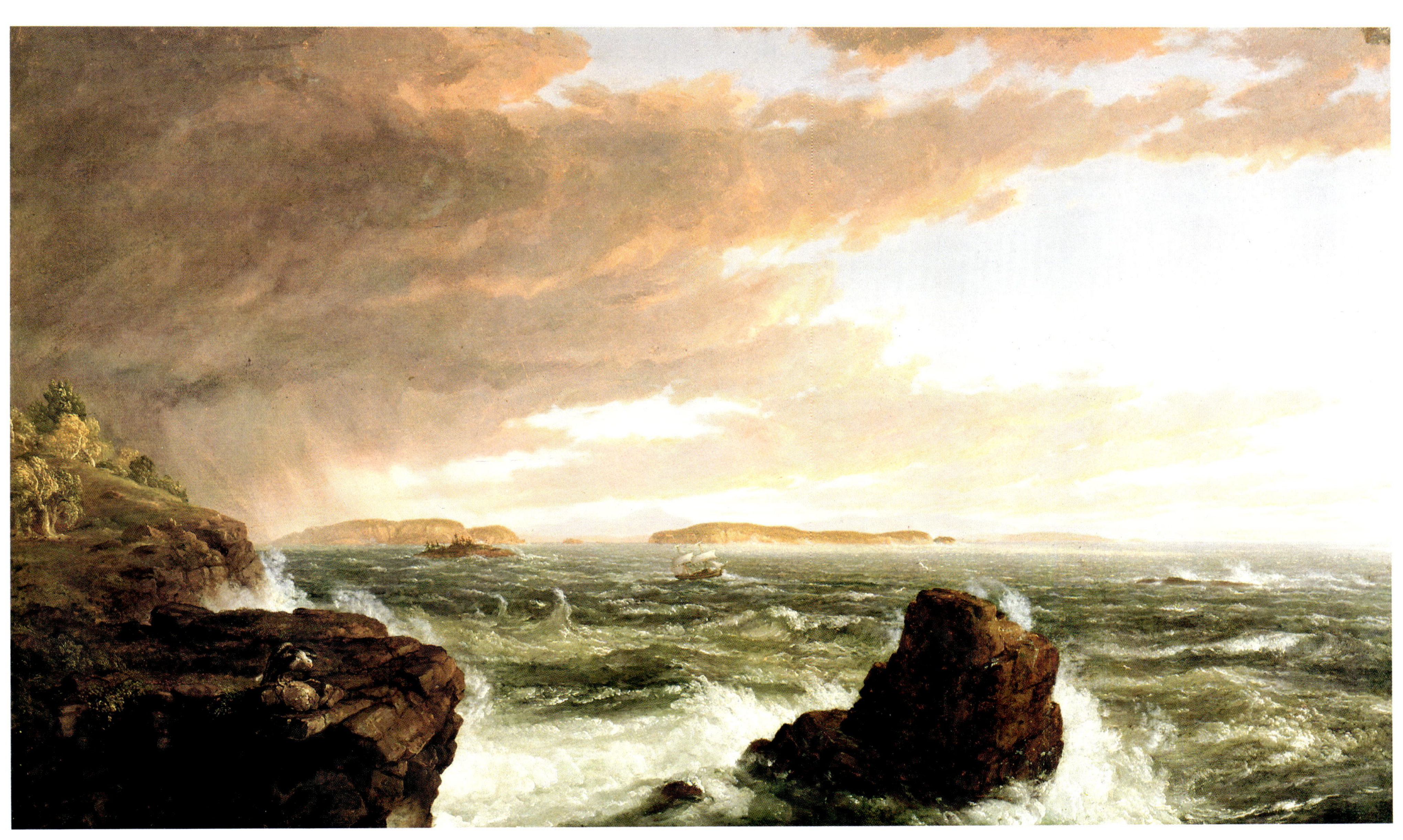

Honoré Daumier

1808-1879 • FRENCH

Orchestra Stalls

c. 1865

DAUMIER NEVER FINISHED this painting, but the heads and torsos thinly washed in oil and turpentine fulfill the artist's concept. Unlike many of Daumier's works, it is devoid of social comment or criticism. It is a subject drawn from common experience and expresses the simple, direct viewpoint of much painting of the nineteenth century. Although *Orchestra Stalls* is unfinished, this very condition is appealing for the insight it gives us into an artist's methods and first steps in creating a painting.

Daumier was one of the world's first lithographers, and he developed a fluid drawing style on the lithographic stone that provided him a livelihood as an editorial artist (or cartoonist, we might say today) for two leading humorous magazines of Paris, *La Caricature* and *Le Charivari*. During his career, he made about four thousand illustrations for these magazines. It was only after 1848 that oil painting occupied him, and most of his canvases were rich in earth tones and muted with low-key color.

Oil on canvas, 23 13/16 x 33 1/4"
The Edwin and Virginia Irwin Memorial, 1960

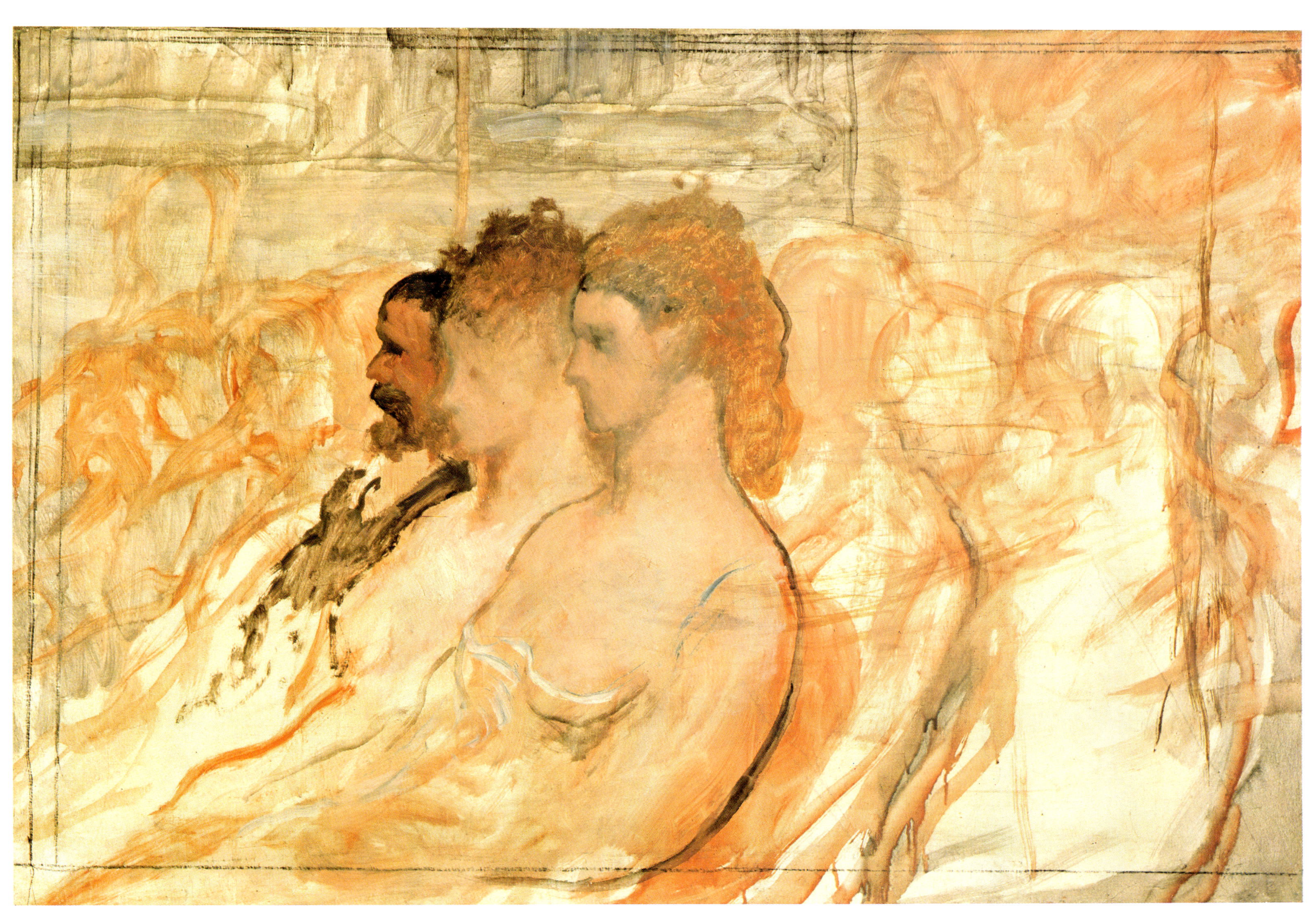

Charles François Daubigny

1817-1878 • FRENCH

The Pond of Gylieu

1853

DAUBIGNY DEVELOPED AN EARLY and keen appreciation of the landscape from his father, who also was an artist, and from a trip to Italy in 1836. From 1838 he exhibited landscapes regularly at the Salon but did not seek the Barbizon environment in the forest of Fontainebleau until 1843. He was better known as an etcher until he was in his thirties, but true fame as a painter was his at mid-century. Although criticized by some contemporaries for his lack of finish in paintings, even those submitted to the Salon, he was both a major member of the Barbizon School and a precursor of the innovative French painting advanced by Monet, Pissarro, and Renoir.

Daubigny's favorite region for painting was near Optevoz, southeast of Lyon, where this painting was done just one year after he worked with Corot. None other than the emperor Napoleon III once owned this placid scene, purchased in 1853 when it was painted, the same year it earned a first-class medal in the Salon. It was considered Daubigny's masterpiece then and probably remains so today. Preliminary drawings of storks and the pond prove the artist's careful study of the composition before setting paint to canvas, but even the completed painting's grainy, rough brush-work retains a freshness that endeared Daubigny to the Impressionists who were influenced deeply by the older man.

Oil on canvas, 24½ x 39¼″
Gift of Emilie L. Heine in memory of Mr. and Mrs. John Hauck, 1940

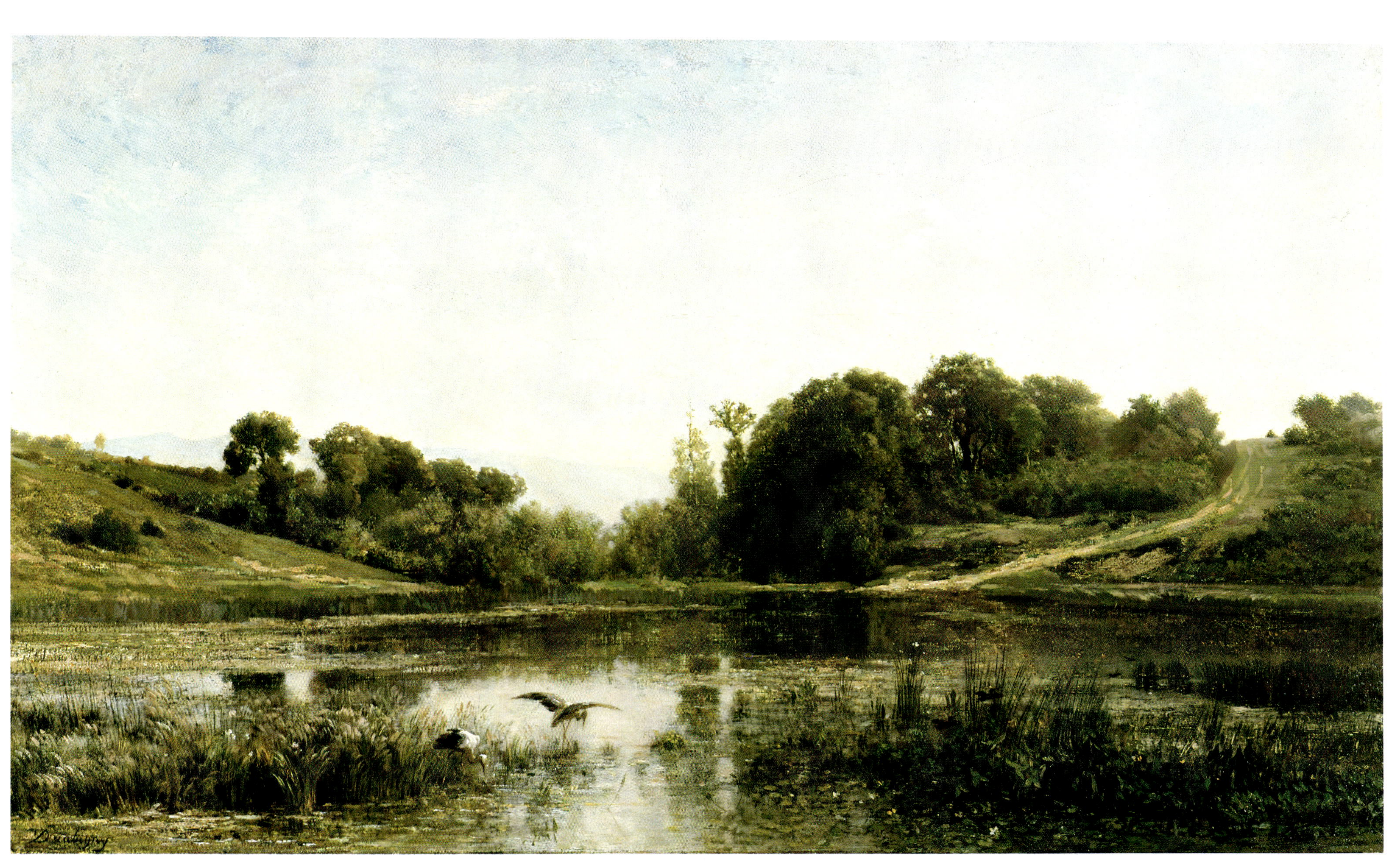

Robert Duncanson

1821-1872 • AMERICAN

Blue Hole, Little Miami River

1851

ROBERT DUNCANSON was the first black artist of America to achieve distinction both in Cincinnati and in broader art circles nationally. By 1842 he lived in Cincinnati, and most of his career was spent in the Queen City until cut short by mental illness and death in Detroit in 1872. He was assisted greatly by Nicholas Longworth, a distinguished businessman, entrepreneur, and arts patron, who provided him with commissions. Duncanson was largely self-taught and primarily a painter of landscapes, although he practiced portraiture and still-life painting as well.

Duncanson's masterpiece is this hymn to nature, his rendering of an actual site on the Little Miami River in Ohio. His placid scene of trees, pool, and fishermen at "Blue Hole" fits the description of it written in 1833 by his contemporary, the artist Miner K. Kellogg—and it looks much the same today. Duncanson probably had access to certain works by artists of the Hudson River School, the dominant school of landscape painting in nineteenth-century America, to which his elegiac style can be related.

Oil on canvas, 28½ x 41½"
Gift of Norbert Heerman and Arthur Helbig, 1926

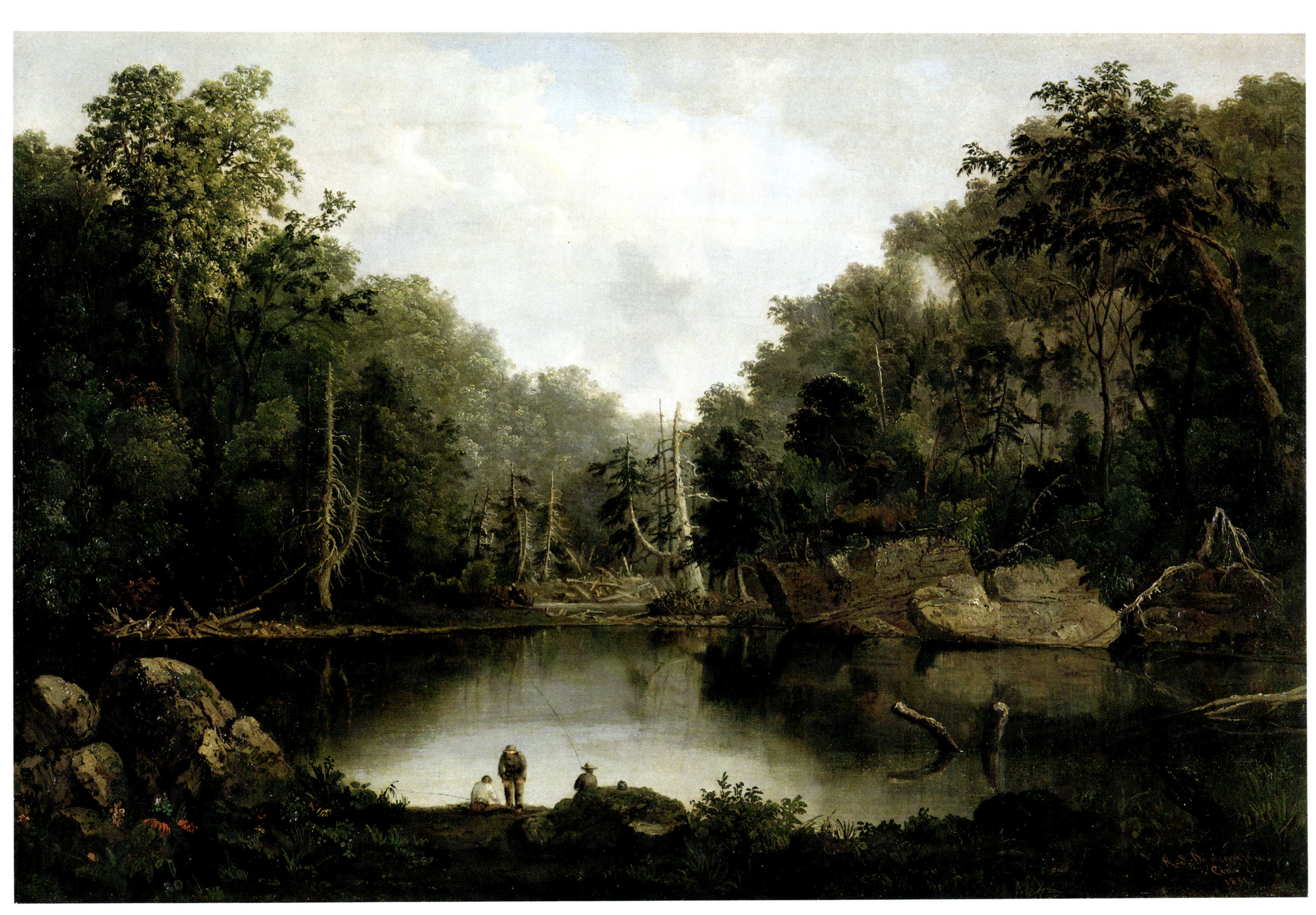

Frederick Edwin Church

1826-1900 • AMERICAN

Falls of Tequendama near Bogotá, New Granada

1854

CHURCH WAS THOMAS COLE'S only pupil. His landscapes vied with his teacher's in popular appeal and were based on panoramic views that excited the imagination and filled the viewer with awe. Church traveled throughout much of the world seeking new subjects, including icebergs in the North Atlantic, jungles in South America, and even Niagara Falls.

As a student of geology and the writings of Humboldt and other scientists, Church was fascinated with natural phenomena. The waterfall he visited in Colombia (once part of Spain's viceroyalty of New Granada) near present-day Bogotá was painted after preliminary drawings were made, properly annotated with color indications and comments on water, rocks, and plant life. Paintings like this one satisfied the educated public's curiosity for faraway spots most would never visit. Such canvases also were vehicles for a widely held theological concern that God can best be understood and seen in nature's most dramatic displays.

Oil on canvas, 64 x 40″
The Edwin and Virginia Irwin Memorial, 1971

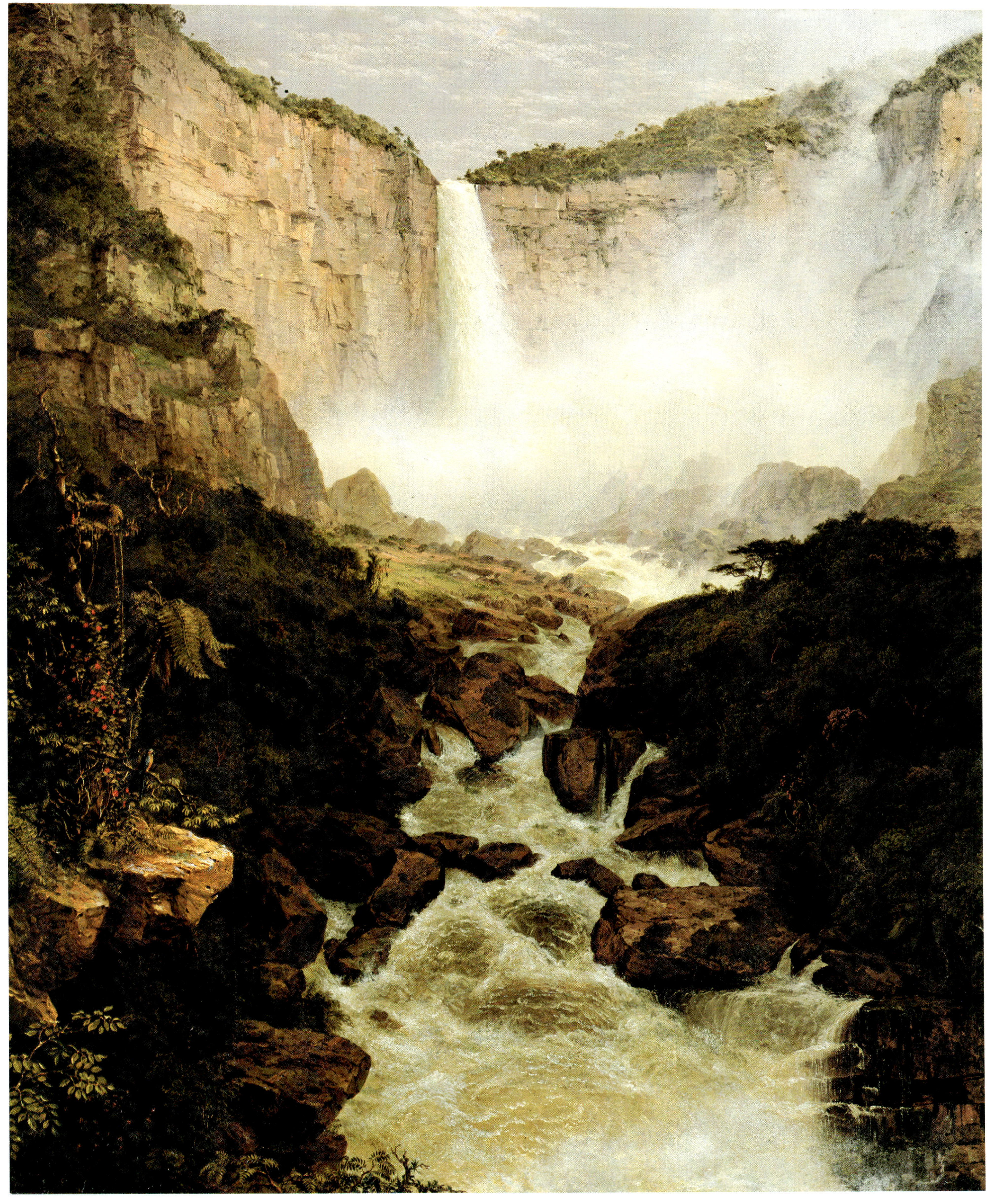

Edouard Manet

1832-1883 • FRENCH

Women at the Races

1864-1865

A VIGNETTE OF ELEGANTLY DRESSED LADIES with their parasols, standing behind a flimsy fence, hardly suggests a setting of a race track with its pounding hooves, the excitement of the approaching horses, the anticipation at the finish line. But the canvas illustrated here that seems so complete as an independent work of art (and is signed and dated) is a fragment of a much larger painting by Manet, now lost. The larger painting was completed in 1864 and dismembered into fragments by 1865, the date on the Cincinnati painting. Today only two paintings, the Cincinnati *Women at the Races* and one once in a Paris collection, are known to survive.

When Manet showed promise as an artist, his father reluctantly allowed him to study painting as a teenager. He rebelled against the standard teaching of his day, seeking dancers and street singers as models for his paintings, which were thought to be vulgar and shocking by his critics. Although the eminent writer, Émile Zola, was a close friend and championed his cause, Manet was frequently rejected by the Salon, the most important juried exhibition for painters in nineteenth-century France.

Manet stemmed from an academic, conservative tradition and always craved official recognition. He embraced Impressionism after 1870 but resented any linkage of his work with that of Renoir, Monet, Sisley, and the other noted Impressionists. His early technique was vigorous and strong, his brushwork dashing, his treatment direct and straightforward. These were radical qualities in mid-nineteenth-century France, and a foretaste of freedom yet to come.

Oil on canvas, 16⅝ x 12⅝"
Fanny Bryce Lehmer Fund, 1944

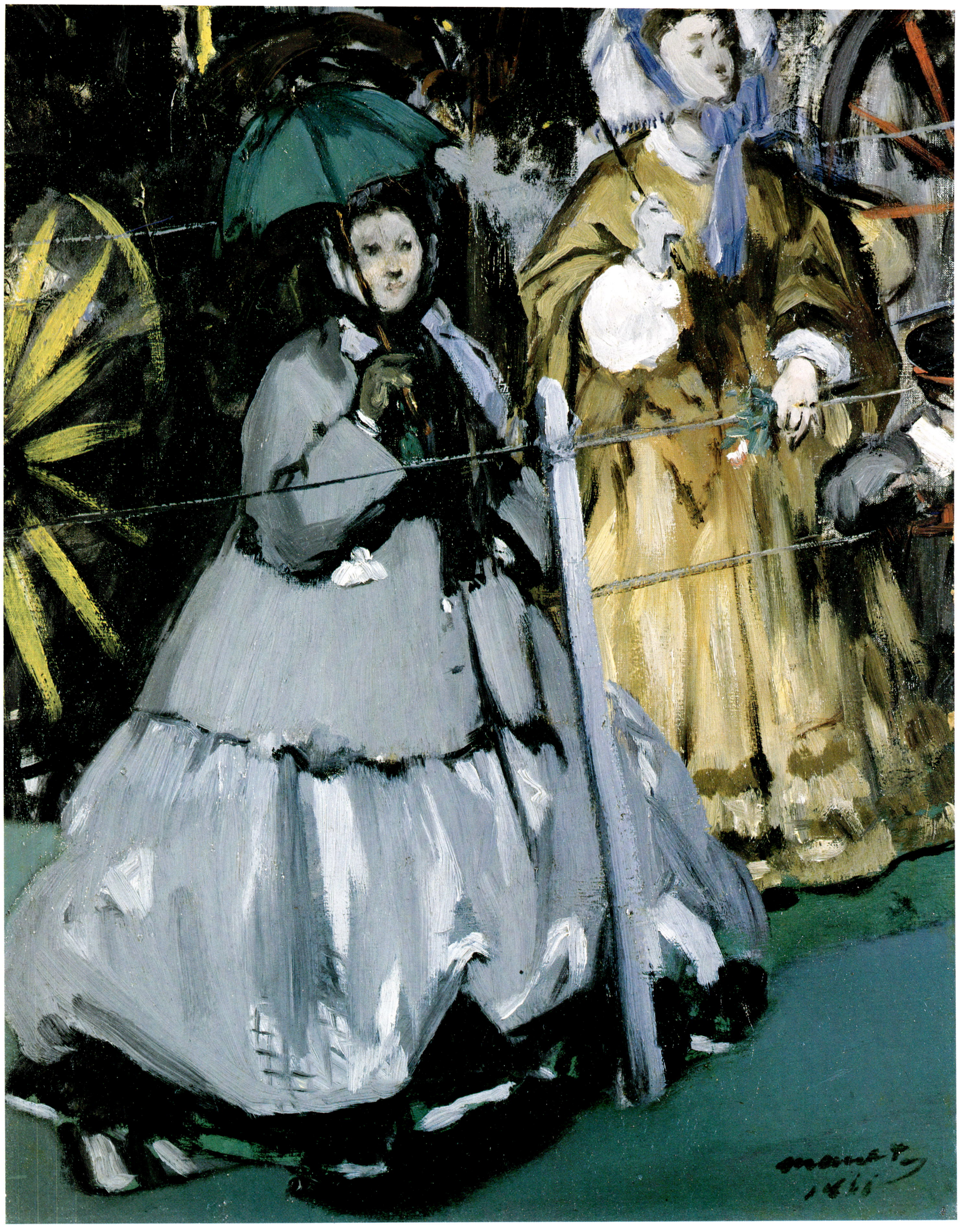

Paul Cézanne

1839-1906 • FRENCH

Still Life with Bread and Eggs

1865

ONE CRITIC HAS CALLED CÉZANNE "probably the greatest painter of the last 100 years." Others have recognized him as the father of modern art. His life was not as dramatic as Van Gogh's, a contemporary, nor fraught with financial deprivation. Cézanne's family was relatively wealthy, and he trained to be a lawyer, but by 1862 devoted himself entirely to painting. As a friend of Pissarro, he became acquainted with the Impressionist artists and even exhibited with them at the first and provocative Impressionist exhibition of 1874.

Veering away from the Impressionists' interest in light and surface, Cézanne sought to model the objects painted on canvas as expressive of the underlying forms of the objects, giving them real structure and body. Still-life and landscape painting gave Cézanne his greatest freedom (they were patient subjects in front of a demanding artist!), as he sought to depict, it is said, the cone, sphere, and cylinder in nature. That is, Cézanne's art was based on a modeling that blended color and tone into something solid, an intellectual exercise that was then translated into a two-dimensional visual experience, the painting.

The Cincinnati painting is signed and dated 1865, one of only six or so paintings bearing both his signature and the year it was painted. Manet complimented him on the beauty of this masterpiece, praising the work for its obvious dependence, too, on Manet's restricted dark palette of brown and black with few half-tones.

Oil on canvas, 23¼ x 30″
Gift of Mary E. Johnston, 1955

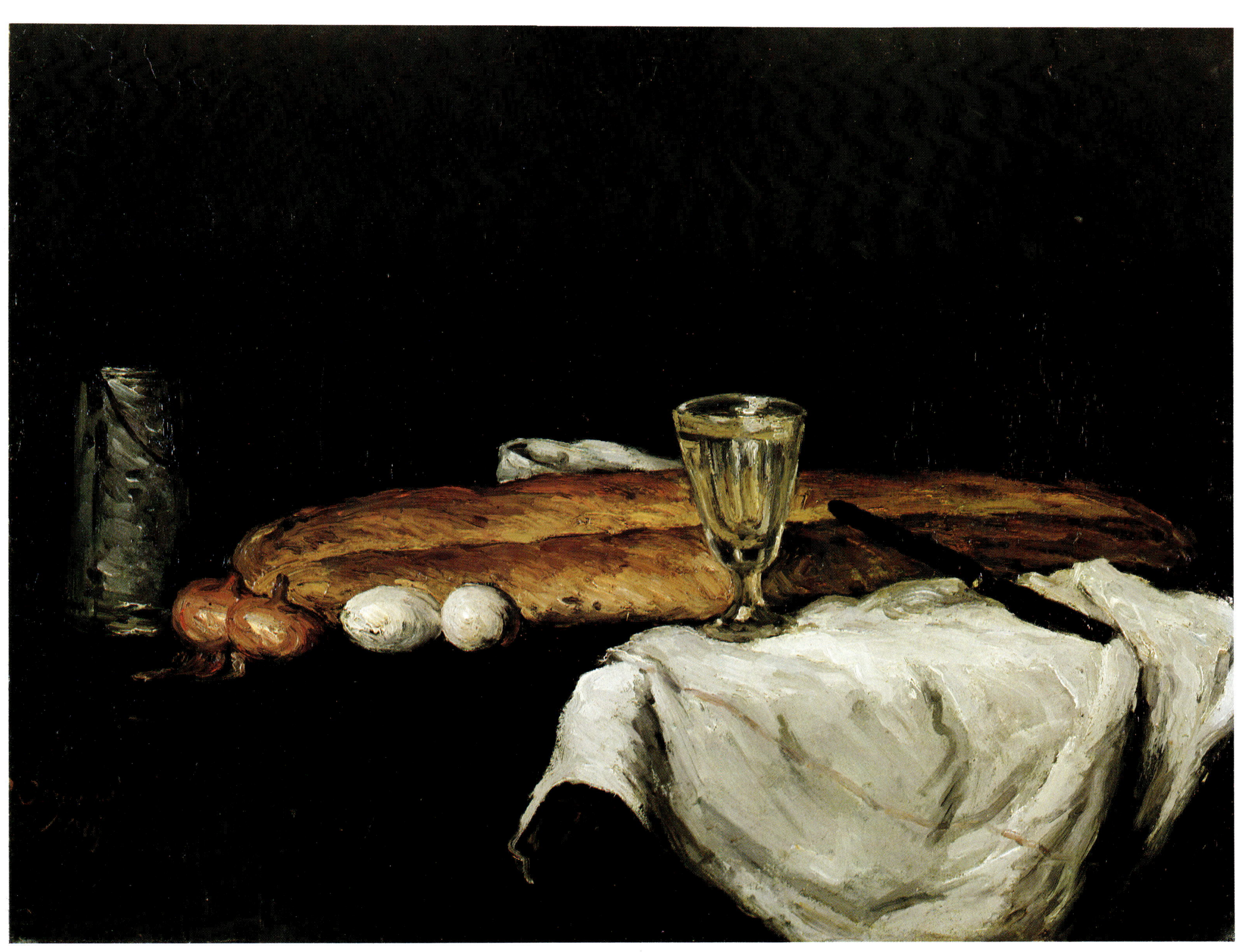

Frédéric Bazille

1841-1870 • FRENCH

The Terrace at Méric (Les Lauriers Roses)

1867

BAZILLE DIED YOUNG, a casualty of the Franco-Prussian War. His wealthy parents provided a life of ease for the artist, who joined the budding Impressionists Renoir, Manet, and Pissarro, whom he helped to support financially and sympathetically. What Bazille's mature development would have been, had he not been killed in action at the age of twenty-nine, is pure conjecture. Based on his sixty or so works in existence, he had much promise and probably would have equaled or surpassed his better-known contemporaries as he led them into Impressionism.

The terrace and garden of the country home of the Bazille family at Méric in southern France, warmed by sunshine and perfumed by oleanders and verbena, interested Frédéric Bazille throughout his tragically short life. Each summer the artist returned to his estate near Montpellier for painting and for reunions with his relatives. The Cincinnati painting was executed in the summer of 1867, perhaps a work intended as a study for his masterpiece, *The Family Reunion*, a scene portraying Bazille and his cousins, brother, parents, and in-laws grouped on the same terrace and shaded by the same trees. He was the first artist among the Impressionists to try to resolve problems of combining group portraiture with figures in the out-of-doors. Brilliant patches of light, rather flatly painted, contrast sharply and produce a clearly defined, intense landscape that has the ghostly image of an unfinished figure (perhaps his cousin Thérèse?) in its foreground. The painting is obviously a study.

Oil on canvas, 21¾ x 36″
Gift of Mark P. Herschede, 1976

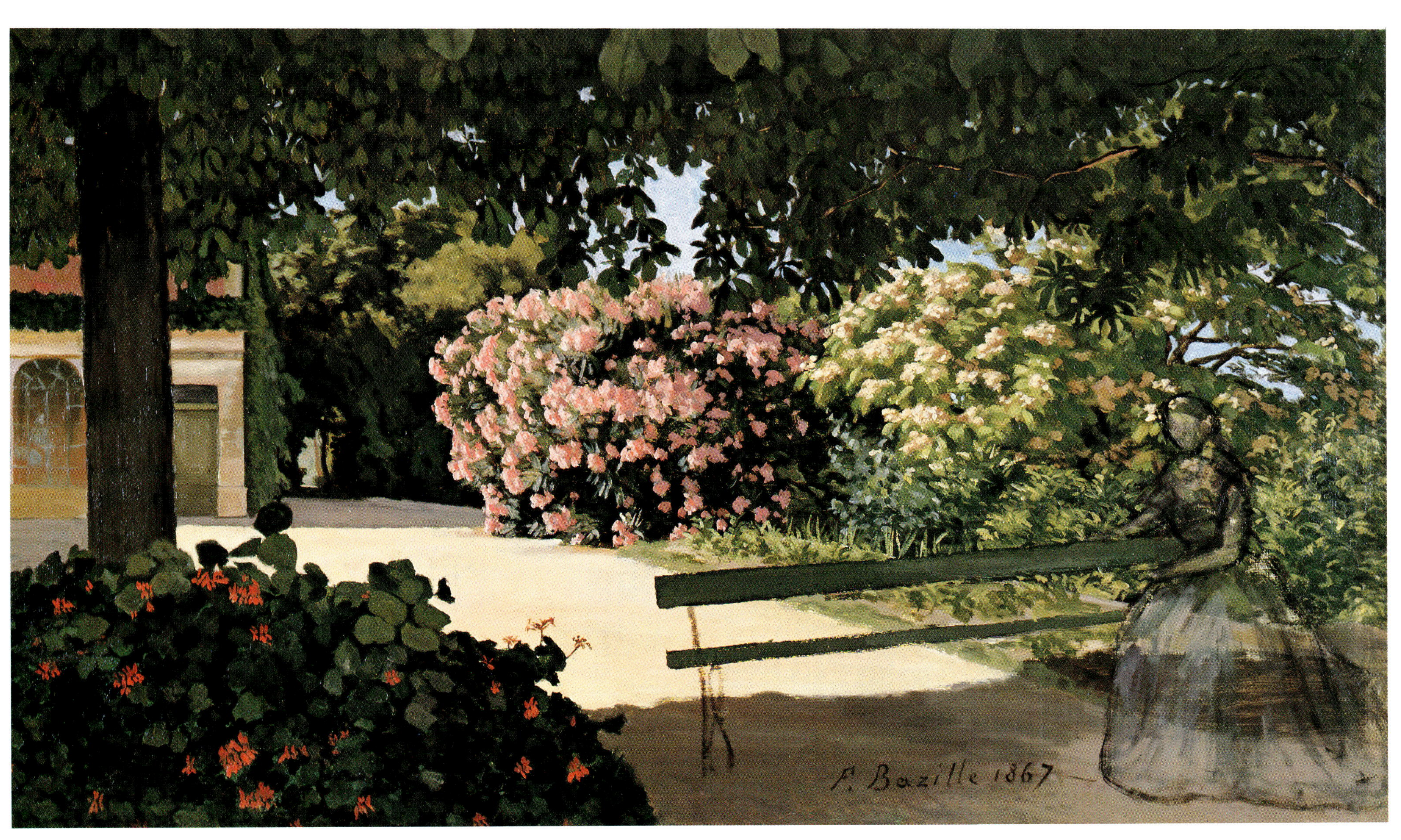
F. Bazille 1867

Mary Cassatt

1844-1926 • AMERICAN

Mother and Child

1889

MARY CASSATT spent most of her life in France and is recognized today as one of America's three most important expatriate artists. Born near Pittsburgh, she studied abroad and in Philadelphia. She was drawn into the circle of French Impressionists by her friend, Edgar Degas, and she exhibited with that group in the 1870s. She became a major American Impressionist and one of the few who enjoyed equal standing with French contemporaries.

Mary Cassatt's interest in children and women as models in her paintings never waned. She captured moods, expressions, and gestures that were preserved in a moment frozen with flat colors outlined with draftsmanly brushwork. A photographic likeness was not attempted, and unfinished areas (note the background and clothes of the woman and child) were deliberately left incomplete. Maternal love and a child's innocence are touchingly depicted in this painting by Miss Cassatt, yet this obviously affectionate interpretation never gives way to mawkish sentimentality.

The painting remained with the artist until her death, as Mary Cassatt resisted repeated offers from the Paris dealer Durand Ruel to purchase it from her. When the Cincinnati Art Museum acquired it from Durand Ruel scarcely two years after the artist's death, its title (translated from the French) was *Baby in blue suit, a finger in the mouth, on the shoulder of a young woman in gray*.

Oil on canvas, 29 x 23½"
J. J. Emery Endowment, 1928

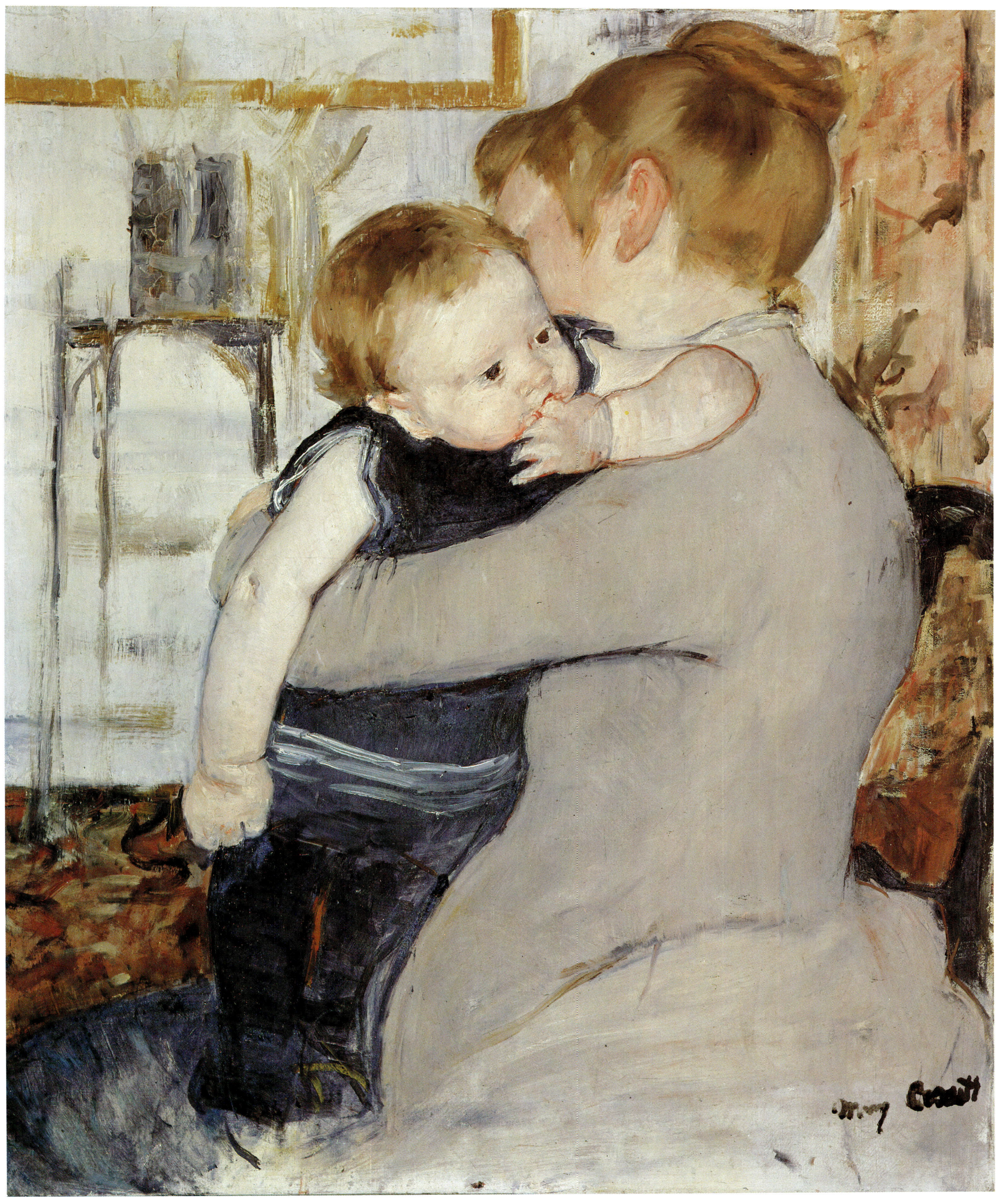

Thomas Eakins

1844-1916 • AMERICAN

Archbishop William Henry Elder

1903

THOMAS EAKINS LIVED AND WORKED in Philadelphia, where he taught painting at the Pennsylvania Academy of Fine Arts until a controversy over the use of nude models in his life drawing classes prompted his resignation from the faculty in 1886. As a young artist he studied in Paris and in Madrid and Seville, often copying great Spanish painters such as Velázquez and Ribera to sharpen his eye and to incorporate into his own work the honest interpretation of character and personality he found in their portraits.

Eakins was a born teacher who encouraged students to draw from the nude model, to learn anatomy, and to paint what was seen, not what was imagined. The public was largely indifferent to his work, perhaps because of his uncompromising realism. He had little financial success as a portrait artist. Eakins is today an American artist of international fame, especially for his penetrating, expressive portraits that influenced the later course of portraiture in the United States.

Shortly after 1900, Eakins painted several portraits of clerics, men it is thought he had met at a seminary in Overbrook, Pennsylvania, through a friend. The seminary was near Philadelphia, and Samuel Murray and Eakins (who had no religious affiliation and apparently was an agnostic) frequently rode out there on their bicycles. Eakins found the clergy's intellect and scholarship appealing, and to his painterly eye, the vestments of the prelates must have harked back to those eloquent portraits of religious officials from Catholic Spain.

Most of his sitters were friends or men and women he asked to pose. The portrait of Archbishop William Henry Elder (1819-1904) was painted in Cincinnati in December, 1903. The artist wrote to a former pupil: "I was out in Cincinnati painting the old Archbishop Elder. I think it is one of my best." The painting won the Temple Medal in 1904 for Eakins, a prestigious award from the Pennsylvania Academy. Archbishop Elder was nearing the end of an active life when he posed for Eakins. His priestly career led him through Civil War battlefields, years of theological teaching, and heavy administrative duties in Cincinnati in reorganizing the diocese.

Oil on canvas, 66⅛ x 41⅛"

Gift of Louis Belmont family, E. F. Hinkle Collection, and bequests of Farny R. Wurlitzer and Frieda Hauck, by exchange, 1978

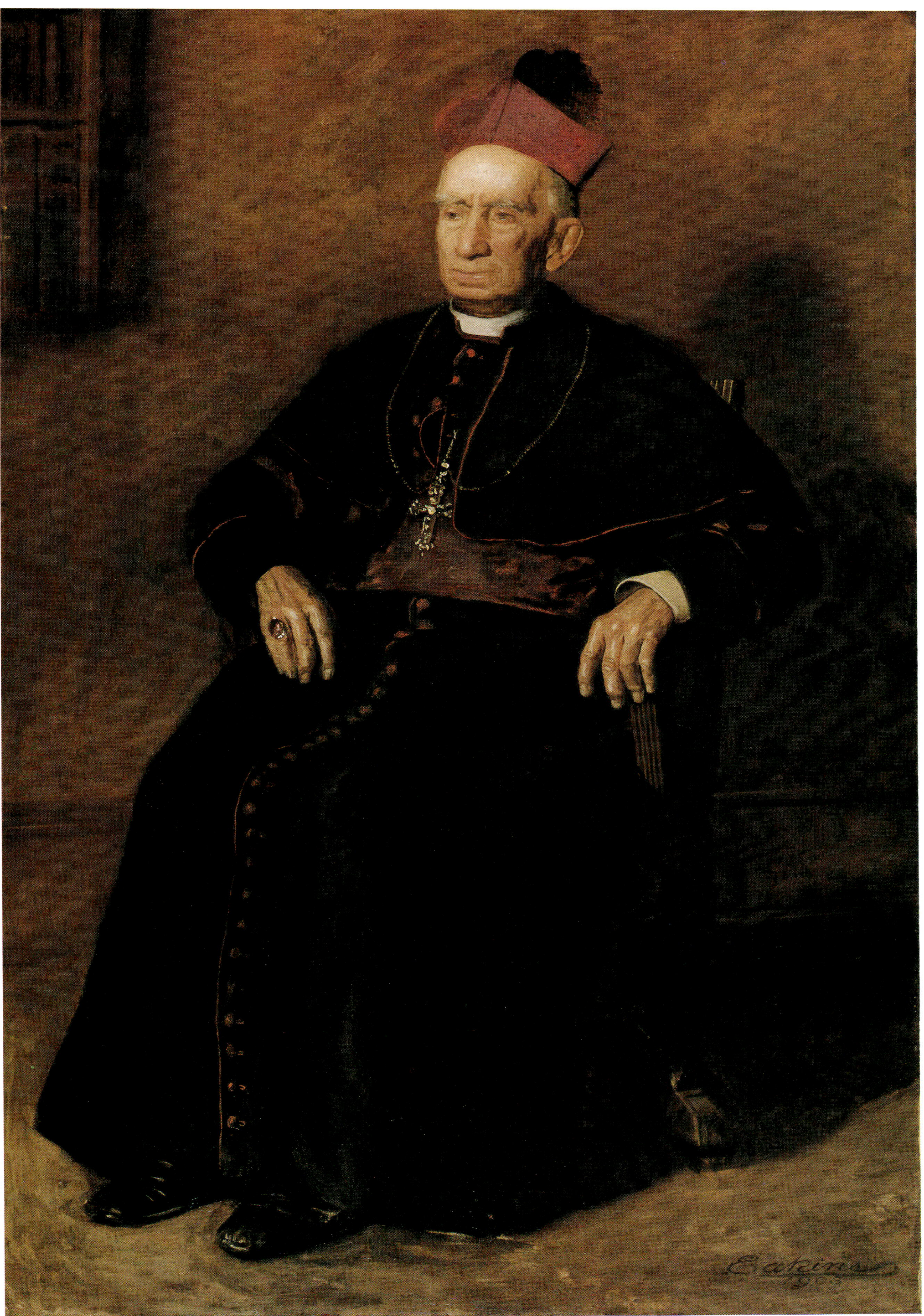
Eakins
1903

Henry F. Farny

1847-1916 • AMERICAN

Indian Camp

1890

FARNY STANDS WITH REMINGTON AND RUSSELL among the most important artists of the West and the American Indian. He was born in France and settled in Cincinnati in 1859. By 1865 his first illustrations appeared in *Harper's Weekly*, and he studied in Europe off and on until establishing himself in Cincinnati by 1874. His studio was described as a "perfect little museum of curiosities," suggesting an interest in collecting objects that might be included in his paintings. Farny was a close friend of Duveneck and Twachtman. After 1880, he narrowed his subject matter to Indians and the West, basing his paintings on frequent western excursions. The American West was a rich lode for artists who recognized its colorful past, the appeal it had to a society barely recovered from its collision with the original Americans' way of life, and the exotic allure of a strange, primitive culture. Farny capitalized on this and brought his illustrator's talent to focus on the West quite sensitively.

Farny was essentially a studio artist. His finished paintings were done from sketches and photographs. *Indian Camp* is a luminous rendering of finely detailed figures (perhaps Sioux Indians) and landscape. It probably is not an accurate depiction of a single camp or scene but a composite. In Farny's best works, such as this one, the narrative element is subdued and a haunting loneliness prevails.

Oil on canvas, 22⅛ x 38⅝"
Bequest of Mrs. William A. Julian, 1949

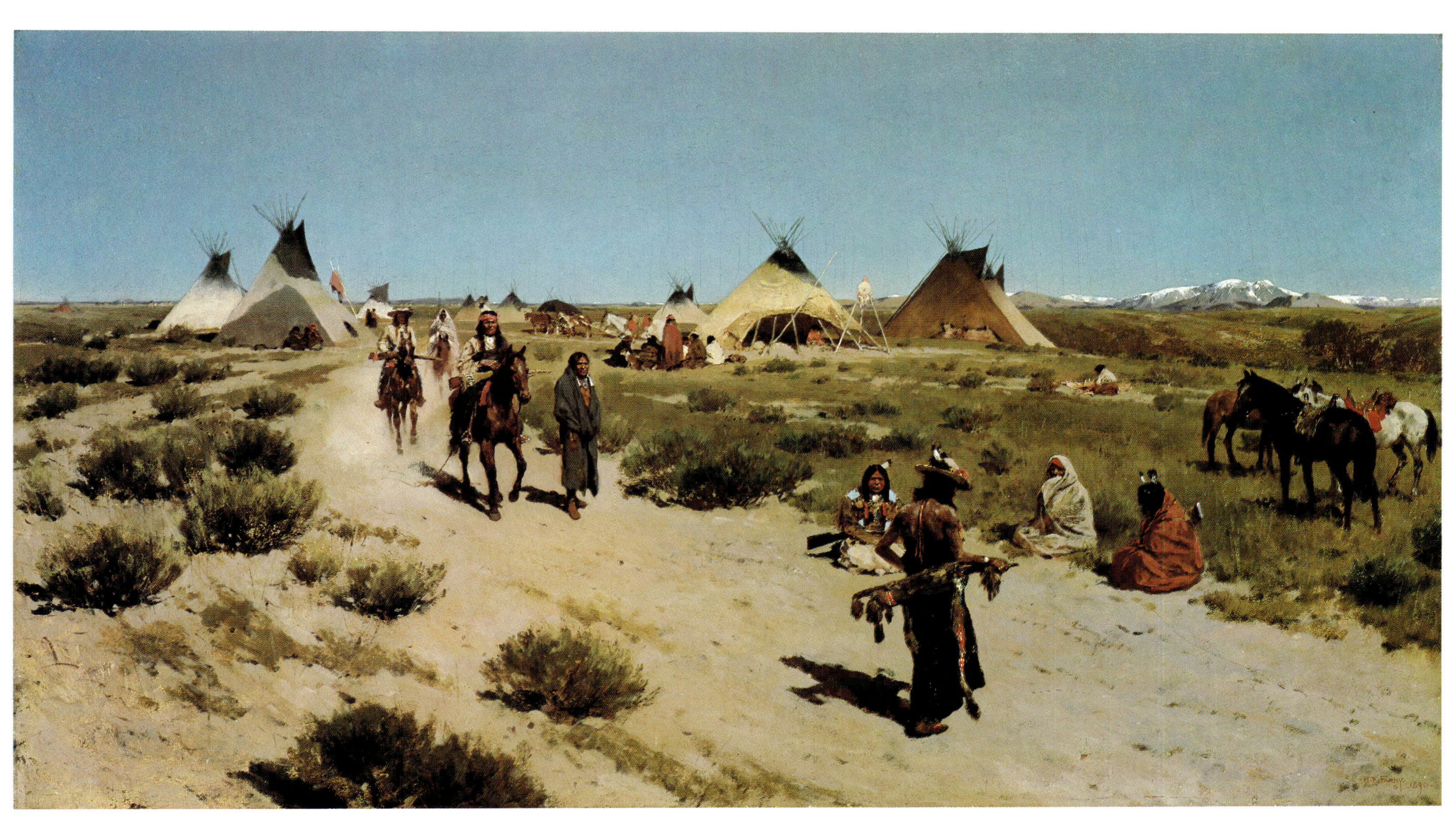

Frank Duveneck

1848-1919 • AMERICAN

Whistling Boy

1872

DUVENECK'S CAREER BEGAN and ended in Cincinnati. In between were years of study abroad (particularly in Munich) and painting expeditions (in Italy and Spain) surrounded by younger artists who were called "Duveneck's Boys." He was a teacher of considerable influence, with revolutionary ideas about painting, insisting that variety in subject matter must be sought, that the depiction of character realistically portrayed with all its flaws was essential, and that brushwork must be strong and vigorous.

Among American paintings, this example of Duveneck's bravura brushwork has become an American icon. It is his best-known work, a touching rendering of a street urchin, painted in Munich shortly after the artist arrived in that German city to study at the academy.

In 1872, this painting would have been considered by many critics to be unfinished or crudely rendered in its thick impasto and slashing brushstrokes. Like much modern painting, however, the *Whistling Boy* extols an act of painting; brushwork is as important as the subject itself. This raffish but charming boy is a model Duveneck preserved forever—his name is unknown to the world; yet he is immortalized on canvas by one of America's great artists and teachers.

Oil on canvas, 27⅞ x 21⅛"
Gift of Frank Duveneck, 1904

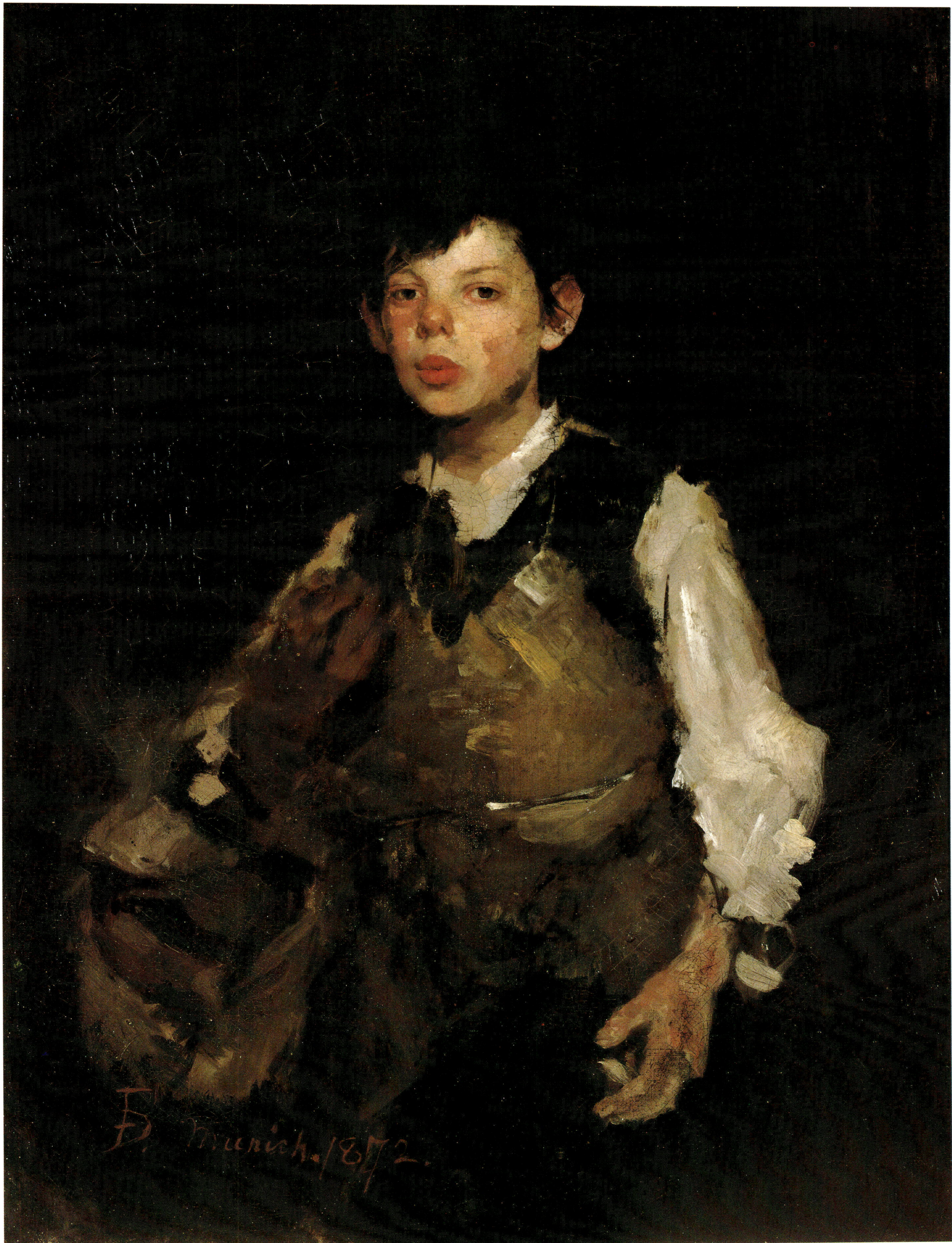

Vincent van Gogh

1853-1890 • DUTCH

Undergrowth with Two Figures

1890

VAN GOGH WROTE MANY LETTERS (usually to his brother, Theo) trying to put into words his innermost feelings and concerns, but ink on paper never could convey the intensity, vision, and struggle always present in his paintings. In late June, 1890, just one month before his suicide in the French town of Auvers-sur-Oise, Van Gogh wrote descriptively of this painting, impressed with its color and structure: "Then I have a canvas 40 inches long and only 20 inches high of wheat fields, and one which is a pendant to it, of undergrowth, lilac poplar trunks and at their foot, grass with flowers, pink, yellow, white and various greens." A few days later, another letter he wrote described the "violet trunks running across the landscape, perpendicular like columns. . . ." The Cincinnati painting's mysterious figures, the acid colors, and slashed brushwork create an emotional statement rather than the objective, detached recording of a scene that a lesser artist would render.

Van Gogh's career and life were brief. His earliest influences were Rembrandt and Hals, and, in the mid-1880s, he explored peasant and worker themes that seemed to be allied with those of Millet, an artist he admired greatly. Interested in the color inventions of the French Impressionists, he visited Paris in 1886, and thereafter his canvases were bold orchestrations of strong color. But Van Gogh's personal life and particularly his frequent bouts with insanity, depression, and melancholia affected his work—or rather his vision—for he always felt inadequate to achieve the expressive power he felt but thought he would never realize. How wrong he was!

Oil on canvas, 19½ x 39¼"
Bequest of Mary E. Johnston, 1967

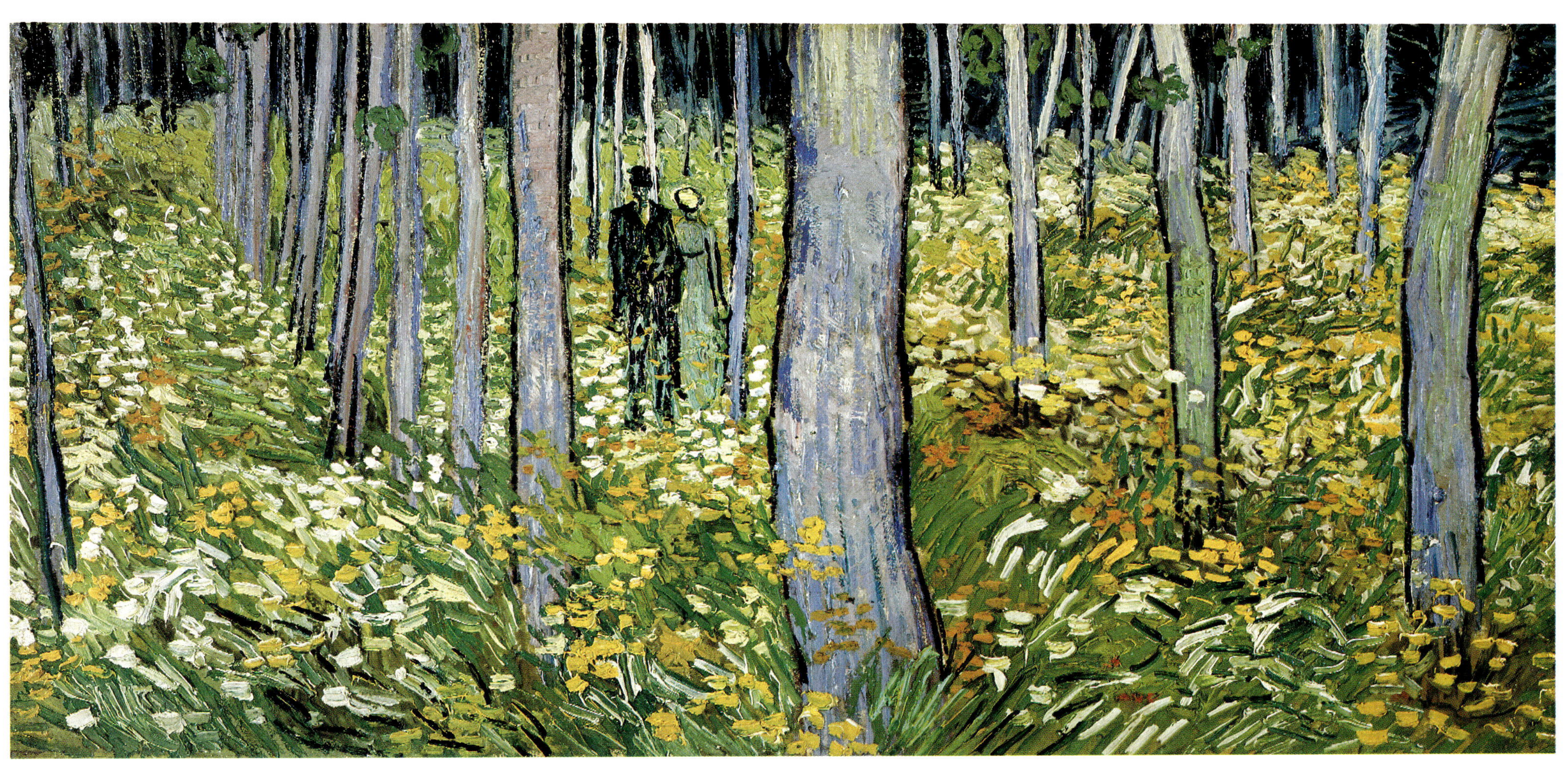

John Henry Twachtman

1853-1902 • AMERICAN

Springtime

1883-1885

TWACHTMAN'S TRAINING as an artist occurred in Cincinnati. The strongest influence in his youth was Frank Duveneck, the teacher and leader of a group of painters that circled around him whether he was in Munich, Venice, or Cincinnati. The dark colors and thickly painted surfaces explored in the 1870s by Twachtman were exchanged for a lighter, blonder palette in the 1880s. The artist's many trips abroad, where he worked in Paris and Florence, must have acquainted him with the dazzling paintings of light by the French Impressionists. By the 1880s Twachtman was an Impressionist.

Seldom has an American artist expressed so beautifully and perfectly as Twachtman did in *Springtime* the concepts developed a decade earlier by Renoir, Monet, and Pissarro. Painted during Twachtman's stay in Paris between 1883 and 1885, this large canvas (similar to another painting in The Metropolitan Museum of Art, *Arques-La-Bataille*) is an exultant proclamation of the break from the brushwork, dark colors, and somber moods generally characteristic of the Germanic influences in late nineteenth-century American painting. From the 1880s to the end of his rather short career, Twachtman was one of America's two or three leading Impressionists. He was one of the original members of the Ten American Painters, a group that included Frank W. Benson, Joseph de Camp, Thomas W. Dewing, Edmund L. Tarbell, Childe Hassam, Willard L. Metcalf, Robert Reid, E. E. Simmons, and J. Alden Weir.

Oil on canvas, 36⅞ x 50″
Gift of Frank Duveneck, 1908

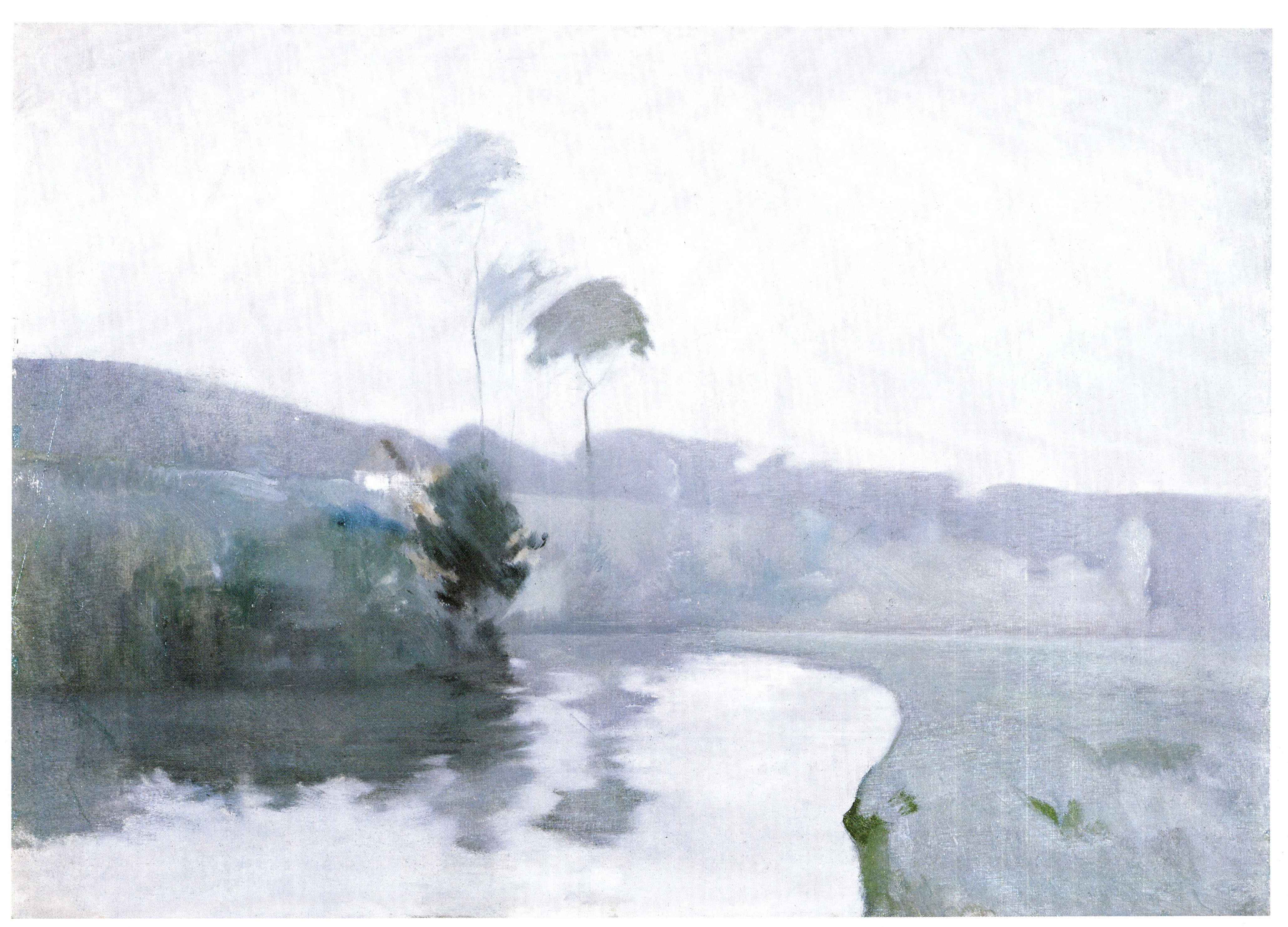

Hans Hofmann

1880-1966 • AMERICAN (b. GERMANY)

Toward Crepuscule

1963

A NEW, VIGOROUS ART—perhaps America's most important contribution to date in the international art scene—emerged in the late 1940s in New York City and became known as Abstract Expressionism. It defined a style of abstract painting that used a loose handling of the medium, masses of color, textured paint, and a kind of ruggedness in shapes spread over the canvas. Dynamic New York became the center for Abstract Expressionism. Many of its practitioners, such as Gorky, De Kooning, Rothko, and Hofmann, were foreign born. Their paintings owed little to European prototypes; they established a new frontier by their own inventiveness and fresh inspiration.

Hofmann was one of the founders of Abstract Expressionism, not consciously a pacesetter but a recognized leader soon after his one-man show in New York in 1944 had blazed a new trail. He was educated in Germany and first worked in the United States around 1934. After emigrating to this country, he soon attracted students. Many of America's best-known painters by the 1950s and 1960s had studied with Hofmann at Provincetown and elsewhere and were influenced deeply by this titanic figure. Hofmann at his most expressive level is seen in the Cincinnati painting, with its "push-pull" of rigid squares of saturated color set against a flowing, heavily textured background. Completely nonobjective and nonrepresentational, this canvas reduces painting to its essence and brings the viewer close to the act of painting itself.

Oil on canvas, 60 x 72"
The Edwin and Virginia Irwin Memorial, 1968

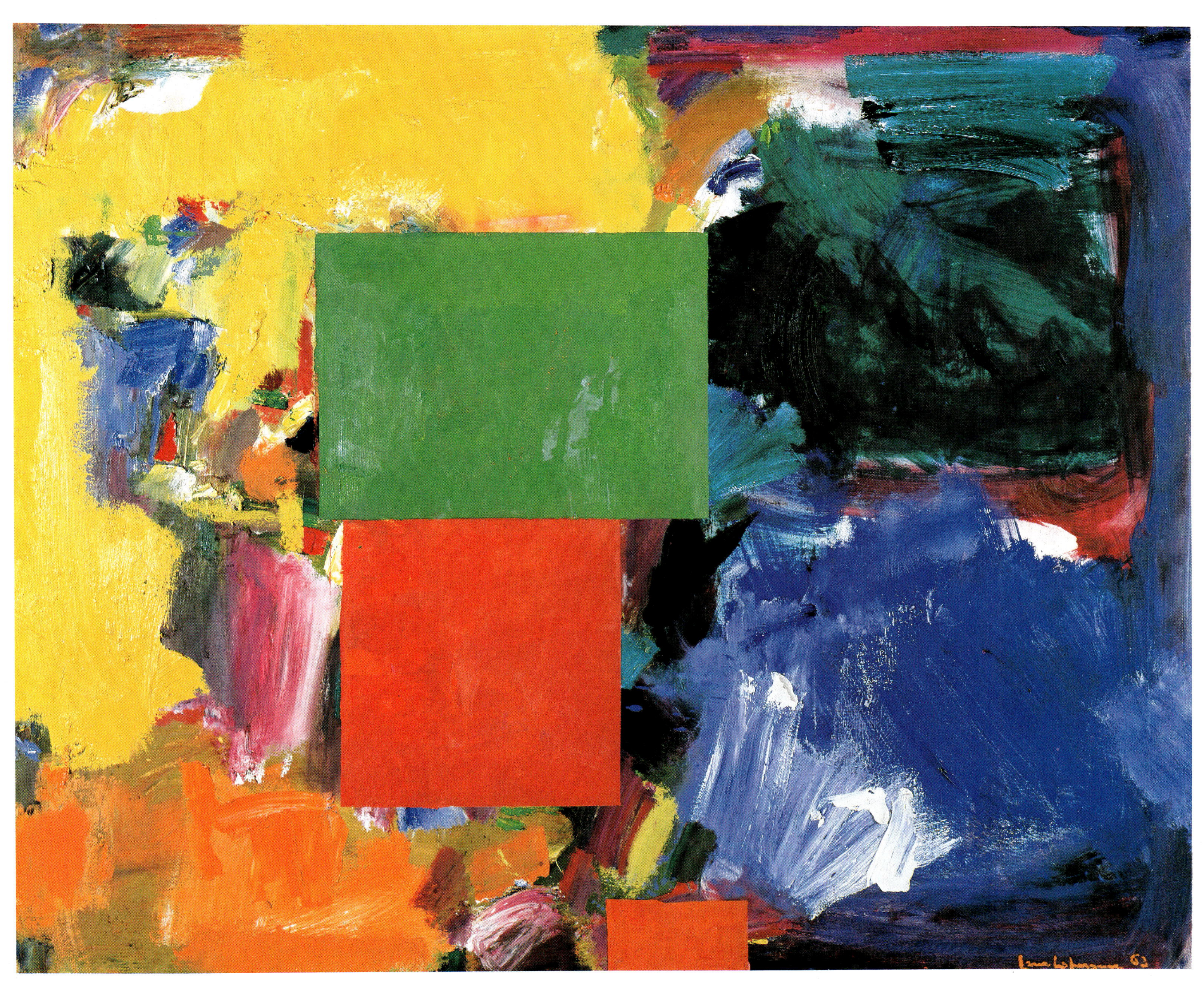

Pablo Ruiz y Picasso

1881-1973 • SPANISH

Still Life with Glass and Lemon

1910

PERHAPS NO ARTIST has been more effective than Picasso in discovering new vocabularies for painting and drawing. Certainly in the twentieth century few artists have approached his talent and invention. Born in Spain, Picasso lived most of his life in France, where his fertile imagination led him through successive styles (the Blue Period, Rose Period, etc.) until the artistic bombshell called Cubism exploded in Europe in 1908.

The term *Cubism* apparently was coined by the critic Louis Vauxcelles, and Picasso, Braque, and Gris were recognized as its leaders. Along with Braque, Picasso began to depict objects or volumes in relationships that did not imitate natural appearances. Color choices, as in *Still Life with Glass and Lemon*, were subdued and nearly monochromatic. In this still life painted at Cubism's zenith, a group of common objects (fruit, bottles, a glass or two) were arranged on a table and reduced to their essentials, reconstituted as geometric forms seen from several angles without relying on the old values of perspective, natural appearance, and chiaroscuro. Cubism probably is the most influential art movement of the past one hundred years, and the Cincinnati painting beautifully illustrates its essence.

Oil on canvas, 29⅛ x 39¹³⁄₁₆"
Bequest of Mary E. Johnston, 1967

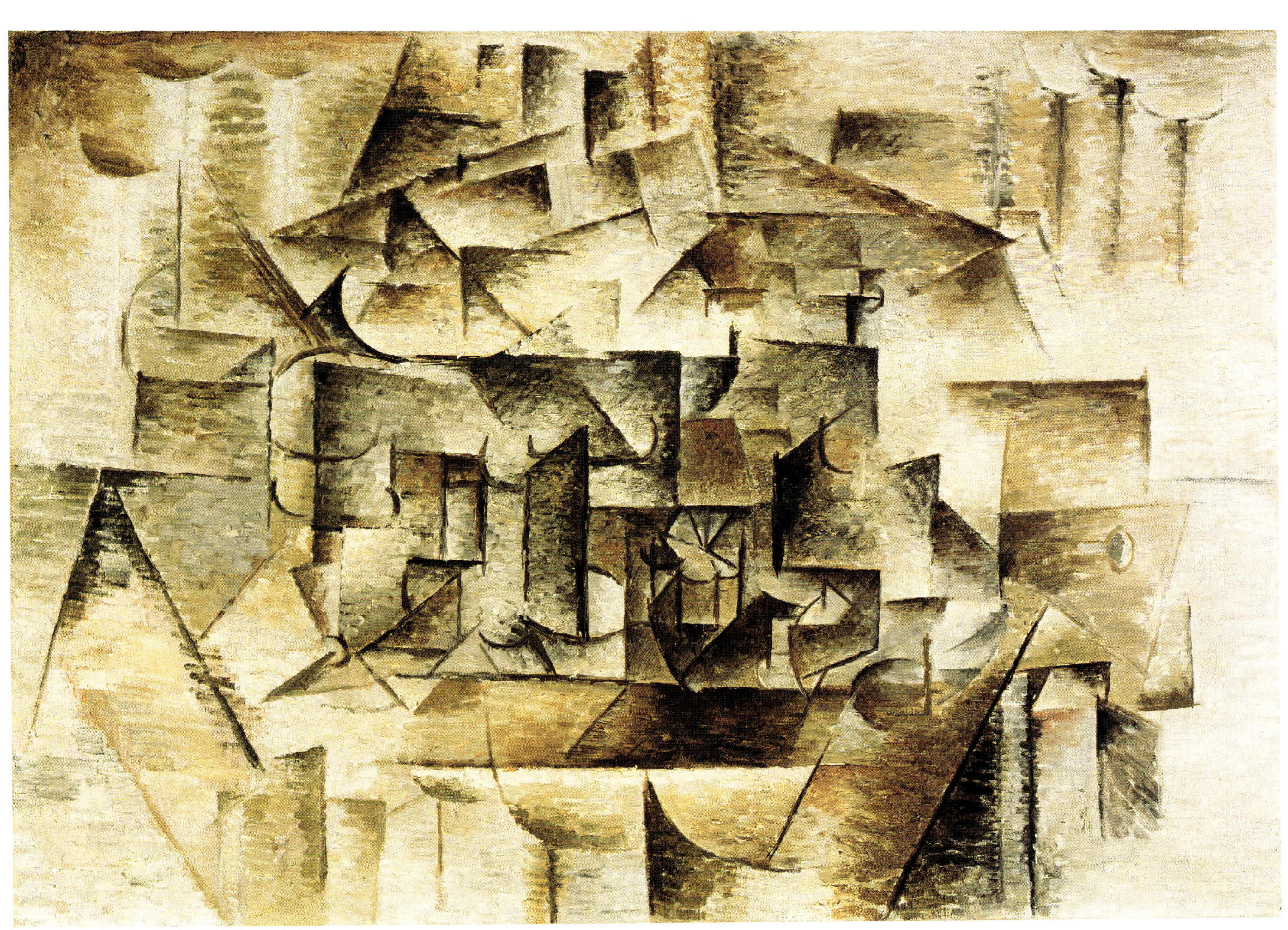

Grant Wood

1892-1942 • AMERICAN

Daughters of Revolution

1932

REGIONALISM, a term applied to artists and writers concerned with American themes and popular culture, was an effective artistic movement in the 1930s that glorified American life and rejected intellectualism and what was called the "aesthetic colonialism" imposed from Europe. Regionalist artists were urged to paint scenes and subjects from the regions where they were born and where they lived. They worked in what they regarded as an heroic style of painting, and expressed in their accomplished draftsmanship readily understood subject matter, with preference for rural topics. Regionalism's strongest members were Thomas Hart Benton, John Steuart Curry, and Grant Wood—all Midwesterners.

Grant Wood was born in Iowa and studied in the Midwest before traveling to Europe after 1920. Before returning to Cedar Rapids where he worked for the rest of his life, contented as a provincial who relished the small-town atmosphere, he admired the precisionist draftsmanship of the Flemish and German artists of the fifteenth century he saw in European museums. But while he accepted the old masters' technique for his slick surfaces and meticulous attention to detail, he rejected European influences otherwise. Frequently, Wood's paintings are touched with irony or are unabashedly satirical, as in *Daughters of Revolution*. Posed before a framed reproduction of Leutze's *Washington Crossing the Delaware*, the three tight-lipped, sour-looking women are caricatures of real people. This painting, along with Grant Wood's *American Gothic*, has become an American icon, certainly one of the nation's best-known works of art and a symbol of significance for its emphatic "Americanism."

Oil on masonite, 20 x 40"
The Edwin and Virginia Irwin Memorial, 1959

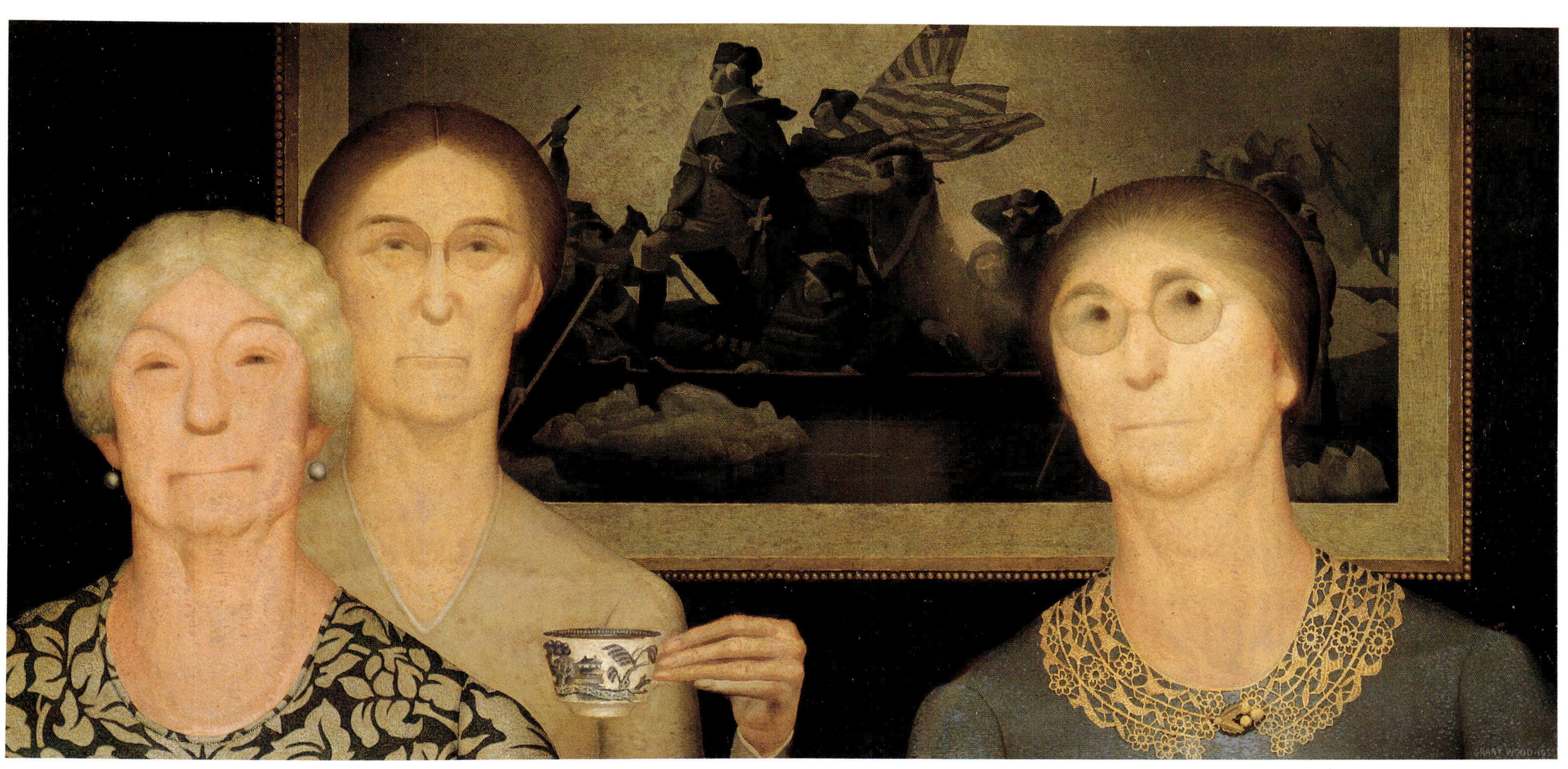

Arshile Gorky

1904-1948 • AMERICAN (b. ARMENIA)

Virginia Landscape

1944

GORKY'S LIFE seemed to move from tragedy to tragedy, culminating in his suicide in 1948. He was one of America's most influential artists and is generally credited as the father of Abstract Expressionism, a major school of painting renowned internationally (also called the New York School) that developed in the decade after World War II.

Gorky emigrated to America in 1920, studied in Boston, Providence, and New York, and was employed, along with many talented artists, in the WPA art project during the Depression. He readily assimilated the styles of Cézanne, Picasso, and Miró and blended in his gleanings from Surrealism before developing his personal, dynamic style by the early 1940s. Beginning in 1943, Gorky spent several summers on a farm in Virginia. There he sketched and painted, drawing inspiration from nature and basing his paintings on the landscape around him. His response was intuitive, automatic. This Cincinnati painting from Gorky's maturity is an example of the exciting new vision that influenced Pollock, De Kooning, Rothko, Motherwell, Hofmann, and other Americans. Abstraction and expressionism in American painting, at least their most important manifestations, emerged as a new style unlike any other, and the first American school of truly international importance was born.

Oil on canvas, 40 x 51″

Gift of Mrs. Benjamin Tate, Peter Gibson, and Horace Carpenter, by exchange, and The Edwin and Virginia Irwin Memorial, 1979

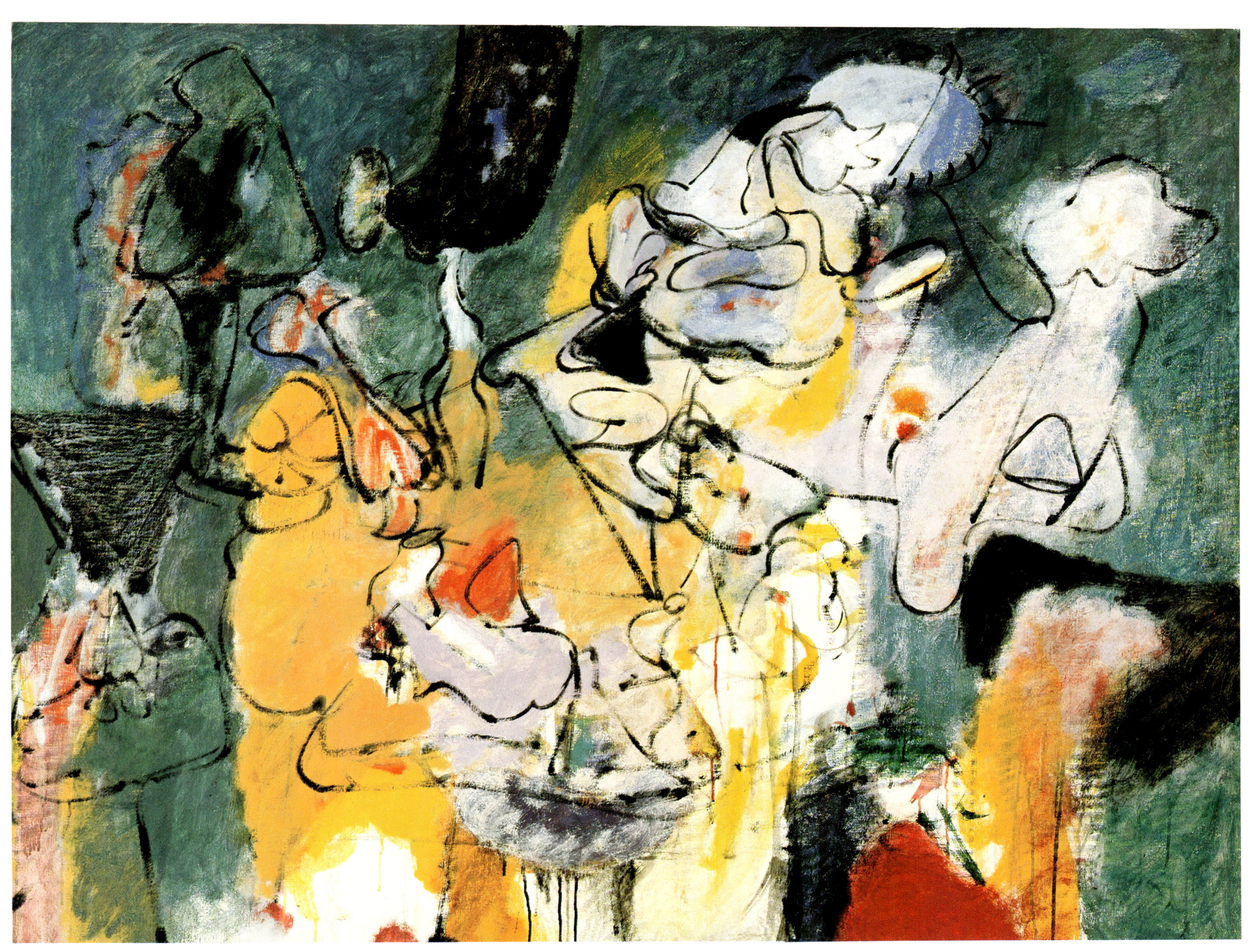

FACING THE TITLE PAGE

Pieter de Hooch

1629-AFTER 1684 • DUTCH

The Game of Skittles

c. 1665

DUTCH PAINTING of the seventeenth century expresses much of what we know today about Holland's economy, politics, religion, and interests during its Golden Age. The people looked lovingly on the land they wrested from foreign control, creating a country of hard-working merchants and tradesmen dependent on the sea. During the Dutch struggle for independence, they competed successfully with the English and Portuguese traders. Their painters were pioneers and explorers, too, for no national school has ever produced more faithful, talented artists who observed what others overlooked: customs and common scenes involving their contemporaries. Their patrons were middle-class businessmen, and pictures were relatively inexpensive. Most paintings were small, designed for the modest-size houses of Holland, and were not limited to religious or mythological subject matter.

Pieter de Hooch worked in Haarlem where he studied, and in Delft where he was influenced by Carel Fabritius and Vermeer. This latter artist was his fiercest competitor, although the charm and domesticity illustrated by De Hooch differs tremendously from Vermeer's tours-de-force of design and color. *The Game of Skittles* freezes a moment on a crystal-clear afternoon where richly dressed men and women play a popular form of bowling at nine pins. The object of the game was to knock down the crowned center "king" pin without disturbing the other eight pins, a feat of considerable skill. The connoisseur who acquired the painting originally from the artist probably engaged in the sport himself. This subject was a successful one for De Hooch, apparently, for two other versions of this painting are known (in the St. Louis Art Museum and in the Rothschild Collection, Waddesdon Manor, England).

Oil on canvas, 29⅛ x 26⅛"
Gift of Mary Hanna, 1950

ON THE BACK COVER

John Singer Sargent

1856-1924 • AMERICAN

Italian Girl with Fan

1882

SARGENT'S PARENTS were prosperous Americans who loved expatriate life in Europe. The young artist was schooled in studios and ateliers in Paris before he exhibited in the Salon of 1877, and by then he was a recognized prodigy of the brush. He traveled extensively, studying Velázquez in Spain and Hals in Holland, finally settling in London in 1885. His circle of friends included other artists (Claude Monet and Auguste Rodin), intellectuals and authors (Henry James), and collectors (Isabella Stewart Gardner of Boston). He was acclaimed as the leading portrait painter of his time, although, like Gainsborough, he preferred to paint landscapes and watercolors. Portraits provided him wealth and social lionization, and he also accepted monumental commissions during his long career, such as the decorations for the Boston Public Library. Toward the end of his life he was offered an English knighthood (which he refused, since he always claimed American citizenship), and even the presidency of the Royal Academy could have been his.

Sargent visited Venice in 1880 and 1882, staying in the Palazzo Barbaro on the latter trip, where presumably this painting was done. The Cincinnati painting is actually a portrait, as the sitter is known. Sargent depicted his model, Gigia Viani, just as she posed for him in Venice during the summer of 1882. Sargent's style then was influenced by the flashing brushwork of Hals. He had mastered the technique of quick execution, and the technical brilliance that beautifully rendered this life-size portrait of a humble peasant girl suited his urbane, stylish sitters equally well.

Oil on canvas, 93¾ x 52½"
The Edwin and Virginia Irwin Memorial, 1972